VICE & VICTORY
(with the emphasis on the former...)

BILL SCHMALFELDT

Printed in the United States of America

First Printing, 2012

Copyright © 2012 Bill Schmalfeldt

ISBN-10: 1481004115

ISBN-13: 978-1481004114

DEDICATION

My Keeper.
My Caregiver
My Protector
My Bestest Buddy
My Heart
My Reason.
My Life.
My Wife.

I LOVE YOU, GAIL!.

WHAT OTHERS ARE SAYING ABOUT "VICE & VICTORY" AUTHOR BILL SCHMALFELDT

"Vice and Victory" is the next natural step for Schmalfeldt, the only trained journalist who has delved into the various dealings of Ali Akbar. The left will howl with laughter and the right with outrage, as the story of a small time conman who seized control of the right wing blogosphere is exposed.

Neal Rauhauser
Internet Warlord

Bill Schmalfeldt is the thinking person's go-to humorist. His ability to draw people into his world is what keeps me anxiously awaiting his insightful works, ranging from biting political satire to his novel about the challenges of living with Parkinson's Disease. It's truly unfortunate that Bill has yet to receive the accolades and attention he deserves. Our readers know he's doing something right; if the side across the aisle feels threatened and angry, a nerve has been touched. Bill knows how to touch the right nerves...with a cattle prodder if necessary.

The Brooklyn Dame, Webmistress
http://borderlessnewsandviews.com

How did an unknown, small-time criminal such as Ali Akbar rise to a position of prominence in the Republican Party's social-media machine? Bill Schmalfeldt connects the dots and provides an answer that will shock readers. Karl Rove for years has appealed to the hearts and minds of America's "values voters." So what kind of values does Mr. Rove exhibit in his personal life? Bill Schmalfeldt lays out the story in gripping detail.

Roger Shuler
The Legal Schnauzer Blog
http://legalschnauzer.blogspot.com/

Muckraking is a dirty job, but someone has to do it. Bill

Schmalfeldt is the Mike Rowe of the blogosphere, plumbing it clean for your entertainment and edification. And he loves his work so much.

Matt Osborne
http://osborneink.com

It's difficult to find a work of non-fiction which reads like a novel, but Bill's books are definitely page turners. He has a unique, irreverent, off-the-cuff style which is both compelling and paradoxically amusing, especially if the subjects are as dark as Bill's tend to be. Put On Your Parky Face is a tragic tale with Bill cast as the subject, but it had me laughing throughout, and it was happy laughter in response to his triumph of spirit.

Jeffrey R. Broido, Kingston, NY

Schmalfeldt goes after these ne'er-do-wells with the restraint of a James Carville and and the reverence of a Roseanne Barr. Despite the fact that these jerks actually rip off Bill's political enemies, he takes them on nonetheless. He seeks to dump justice on scumbags from a great height, he pulls no punches (or kicks, or head-butts) and heeds not their petulant whines and threats. I wouldn't want to get on Bill's bad side. Ever. That's why I'm writing this blurb.

Alex Brant-Zawadzki
Huffington Post Tea Party Correspondent

CONTENTS

ACKNOWLEDGMENTS

I've done much more than that old bore, Delilah!
I took the curl out of the hair of a millionaire
There's no trick gettin' some hick who is cool Just a little warmer
A little brains-a little talent With the emphasis on the former!

Lola from "Damn Yankees"
Lyrics by Richard Adler

Thanks to the people who helped gather the info for this book. The unnamed writer at Breitbart Unmasked and Exposed Politics. To Matt Osborne, Alex Brant-Zawadzki, Melissa Brewer and others who prefer to remain nameless. To nefarious right wing blogger Larry Sinclair, with whom I agree on nothing, for going out on a limb for what he thought was right. To Roger Shuler at the Legal Schnauzer blog for the bravery of being a liberal living in Alabama. To the Brooklyn Dame for allowing me to write in her wonderful blog, Borderless News and Views. Also to Barbara Broido for the frighteningly accurate drawing of me on the "Other Books Written By" page and on the back cover. To my readers at the former Liberal Grouch blog, now doing business as "The Patriot-Ombudsman" at http://patriot-ombudsman.com.

And to you, for reading this.

I thank you!

FOREWORD

Never in all my years as a professional observer of the human condition have I encountered someone with such a huge ego, with such astounding hubris and with so little reason for it than I have in the person of Ali Abdul Razaq Akbar.

If all you knew about Akbar was what you read on his Twitter feed, you would be justified in believing that he will be next in line to be the next chairman of the Republican National Committee. If you read nothing about him but his own Facebook writing, or his absurdly-named "Viral Read" blog, you would be excused for thinking, "Here is a man of substance, someone who knows what he's talking about, someone deserving of respect and attention."

If that's all there was to read about Ali Akbar, then he might have a reason for that huge ego and the hubris of Julius Caesar.

The problem is, there IS more to read about this 27-year old, scrawny, bespectacled politico. It's nothing he wants to talk about. In fact, if you ask him about any of this, he will lie to you. But the proof is right there, on paper, and in the pages of the book I will be making available to the public in time for Cyber Monday after Thanksgiving.

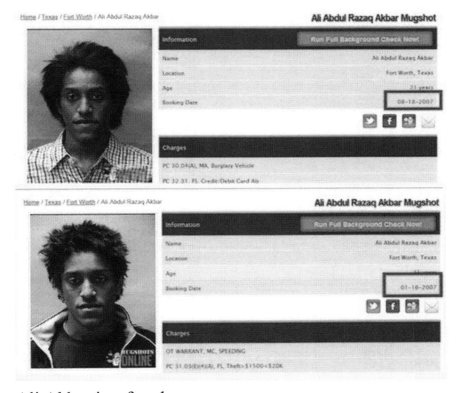

Ali Akbar is a fraud.

Ali Akbar is a convicted criminal.

Ali Akbar is a failure.

Ali Akbar is an inveterate, pathological liar.

In the book, we follow Akbar's career, from his plea deal for crimes including stealing from an old Fort Worth woman, breaking into a man's van, stealing and using his debit card; to his days as a paid hack and liar for the John McCain campaign in 2008. We follow his footsteps from Texas to Georgia, where he went to work for a charismatic Republican congressional candidate named Ray McKinney — who Akbar guided to a loss in the primary election in 2008. With that defeat behind him, Akbar moved up the coast to steer independent candidate Rob Hoffman's congressional campaign — which had successfully pushed the Republican party's choice out of the election — to a solid defeat by the Democrat. With yet another "L" in his column, Akbar went back to help McKinney in Georgia where he piloted McKinney's electoral airplane into the side of a mountain in 2010, leading to yet another loss. McKinney has stopped trying. But even being evicted from his Savannah, Georgia, apartment didn't stop Akbar.

He had no job, no education (he lied to the Dallas Morning News about his education, but the registrar at the University of North Texas says he only attended one semester in 2005), and a trail of losing candidates in his wake, we explore theories as to how Akbar "took over" the conservative blogosphere. Who helped him? Who financed him? How did he keep body and soul together with no job, no education, no prospects. Did he have a sponsor?

We explore the rumor that Akbar did, indeed have a sponsor — so to speak — in the person of Karl Rove. This is based on the writings of others as well as our personal observations, capped off with this otherwise inexplicable e-mail we received from the online "gift store" Zazzle last summer.

Thank you for allowing us to be of service to you.

Subject
Public Product Inquiry: 176147633195511686

Discussion Thread

Response Via Email(Mike) - 07/02/2012 03:43 PM
Hello Zazzler,

Thank you for being a Seller at Zazzle.com!

We would love to offer every design that our users submit, however we must abide by all applicable laws and standards as well as our own content guidelines and copyright policies.

Unfortunately, it appears that your products titled, "pretend time is fun", does not meet Zazzle's Acceptable Content Guidelines. Specifically, your product infringes upon the intellectual property rights of Karl Rove.

Zazzle has been contacted by by representatives by Karl Rove & Co., www.rove.com, and at their request, to remove designs that may infringe upon their rights from the Zazzle Marketplace.

We are sorry for any disappointment, but hope you will understand our position in this regard. For future reference, please review Zazzle's Acceptable Content Guidelines at: http://zazzle.custhelp.com/app/answers/detail/a_id/143.

If you have any further questions, please don't hesitate to contact us.

Thanks for using Zazzle. We look forward to seeing more of your creative designs!

Best Regards,
Mike
Content Management Team
Zazzle, Inc.

Customer By Email (Zazzler Groucheteria) - 07/02/2012 03:41 PM
Again, I have to ask, who owns the picture? Whose intellectual property did I violate if I created the graphic?

This is the image Rove claimed "intellectual property rights" over.

Akbar wearing an Obama mask, waving $20 bills in Karl Rove's face? Yeah. We can see why Rove would claim intellectual property rights to such an image.

With SOMEONE paying his way, Akbar left his many electoral failures behind him and hooked up with his current partners in fraud.

Aaron Marks, former CEO of a company that boasted of "unprecedented success" when nine of the 15 candidates listed on their website as "success stories" were horribly beaten in their elections.

Devon Wills, a childhood friend of Akbar whose credentials to be a "Director" of the National Bloggers

Club included the fact that he was a personal shopper at J Crew before he became the CEO at Wills Group LLC, which defines itself on Facebook as "ayoung boutique east coast-based public relations firm looking to serve as the medium between clients, vendors, marketers, and ultimately consumers. In a world, growing with an emphasis on localization and direct response, sometimes a second set of hands is needed. We hope to fill that need. Our focus remains maximizing the reach of your brand through traditional, as well as digital means." Here's the website.

Contact hello@thewillsgroupllc.com

Copyright © 2011 The Wills Group, LLC.
All Rights Reserved.

That's it. That's the whole website. Nice logo. Nothing else. Not bad for a one-time personal shopper. There is only one entry on the Wills Group Facebook page. It was posted on June 6, 2012.

"I am asking for access to the Articles of Incorporation for your nonprofit, The National Blogger's Club. Ali Akbar refuses to release this information without getting details from me which are not legally allowed. Because he has been convicted of credit card fraud in the past, I do not trust him with my details.

"He says he 'need my information' for his lawyer. I know this is not accurate. He will not even disclose the name of his lawyer.

"I am asking you — you seem like a nice kid — to point me in the direction of his attorney or the registered agent of your nonprofit corporation."

We can find no information about young Mr. Wills that points to any business or political acumen. But, hot dog! He was listed as one of the "20 Hottest Conservative Men in the New Conservative Media" by Gabriella Hoffman in Right Wing News. #9 in fact!'

Devon Wills — only eight men in the new conservative media hotter than he!

Moving on, no discussion of Akbar's enterprise would be complete without a mention of **John Dennis Pedrie**, a childhood friend and director of the National Bloggers Club whose claim to fame was that he worked until 2010 at the Onyx Ice Arena as an Ice Rink Maintenance Man. So he went from Ice Maintenance worker to Vice President of Technology and Development at Vice & Victory, which is another Ali Akbar creation, to one of the Directors of The National Bloggers Club. Wow, sounds like he has some real corporate experience behind him.

Need a Zamboni driver? Pedrie's your man!

Of course, since the foundation of the Vice & Victory agency (which, like the Wills Group, LLC, consists of a website with a logo — and nothing else), Akbar has linked up with such unsavory characters as

Robert Stacy McCain, kicked out of a Seventh Day Adventist enclave for racist remarks and now writer of a blog called "The Other McCain".

Aaron Walker who blogs as Aaron Worthing on a blog called Allergic 2 Bull, in which he raises money on the claim that he lost his job due to the "terrorist threats" of a person who outed him as the creator of a "Everyone Draw Mohammed Day" blog. The person who fired him did wonder about the sanity of a person who would willingly invited the attention of Islamic extremists, but the bottom line says Walker was fired because he was a crappy lawyer.

Lee Stranahan, who along with his buddy Brandon Darby (he was #1 on Ms. Hoffman's list of Conservative Hotties!), blogs and podcasts about the evils of liberalism, stoking fears of a concept known as "swatting" in which police are sent to your home on the basis of an invented threat — much like Stranahan sent Howard County police to the author's home on Sept. 1, 2012 with a trumped up charge that I had threatened to murder, rape, then eat the corpses of his wife and children (or other some such nonsense, which the nice police officer laughed at when he read it on our computer screen).

Patrick Frey, an assistant district attorney in Los Angeles County, California (for now, anyway) who seems far more concerned with helping Aaron Walker prosecute his endless series of lawsuits than he is at prosecuting the criminals in his jurisdiction.

And the list goes on. But for all the liars, freaks, slackers and goofs mentioned above, none can approach Ali Akbar for sheer, unwarranted ego and hubris.

He has never supported a winning candidate. The first electoral effort of the new "Vice & Victory" was to support the candidacy of Jonathon Snyder for the presidency of the College Republican National Committee. Snyder lost in a landslide. Akbar railed against Mitt Romney with his "NotMittRomney" website, until Romney won the nomination. Then, he was a full-throated Romney supporter, predicting a landslide win for Romney all the way past 10pm on Election night. And now, he has started a new Facebook page dedicated to "stopping the second term," reinforcing the exact meme the majority of the electorate soundly rejected on Nov. 7, 2012.

This book will tell you almost everything you need to know about Ali Akbar. If you are a liberal, you will howl with laughter at some of it. If you are a conservative, you will either shake your head sadly or your fist in rage at the author for daring to say such bad (and provable) things about your skeezy little hero.

Either way, buy the book.

Oh, Ali? I'll gladly send YOU a *SIGNED* COPY — if you ask for one.

1 IF AT FIRST YOU DON'T SUCCEED

Bill Schmalfeldt <patriotombud@comcast.net>
To: ali@vvclients.com
I'm writing a book about you, so you may as well tell your story.

November 12, 2012

Dear Mr. Akbar:

Welcome to the first chapter of the book I have started writing about you today. I am compiling all the information past and present that I've dug up about you, compiling it with information others have written about you, contacting people in your past who have worked with you, and am making a good faith effort to tell the whole story about you.

That is the reason for this e-mail.

As the reader will see as they progress through this story, you have done nothing but prevaricate and stall through the past six months as I've tried to get basic information about you. As you will recall, our tete-a-tete began in early June when I tweeted you about your National Bloggers Club, Inc. All I wanted at that time was the Employer's Identification Number that every legitimate 501©3, which the NBC, Inc., claimed to be, is required by the IRS to make publicly available on request. You may recall that your first response was to direct my inquiry to your lawyer. I tweeted you again and said that what I was asking for is not something I should have to get from a lawyer, that as CEO and President of the NBC, Inc., you should be able to comply with such a simple request as providing an EIN.

You responded by blocking me.

The reader will see through this story that your dealings with everyone -- supporters and foes alike -- have been a long string of lies, half-truths and twisted logic.

In this story we will review:

1. Your early life in Texas.
2. Your arrest in Fort Worth for a variety of crimes.
3. Your plea deal.
4. The immediate aftermath of your conviction.
5. You move to Georgia.
6. We will discuss how you were able to travel the east coast working first for Ray McKinney, then Rob Hoffman, then Ray McKinney again even though you were evicted for non-payment of rent from your Savannah, Georgia apartment.
7. We will discuss your rise to the head of the Vice and Victory agency.
8. We will explore your rumored relationship with Karl Rove.
9. We will spotlight your using donation money, according to Larry Sinclair, "for cigars and men who liked poker."
10. We will write about how you detested Mitt Romney until he won the nomination, and then how you were absolutely certain he would win, until he didn't.
11. We will wrap up with your new effort to do the very thing the majority of voters rejected: Dragging your feet and "Stopping the Second Term."

This story will be told.

Whether or not it will be told with your input is entirely up to you.

This is your final chance, Mr. Akbar. I have reached out to you many, many, many times in a gentlemanly fashion to ask you to speak for yourself. But you continue to hide, to insult me through your lickspittle Robert Stacy McCain, to motivate others to try to take down my Twitter account (which, I should mention, I reported to Twitter earlier today).

Would it not just be easier to make yourself available to answer a few questions than to have a book written about you, a book I have ever reason to believe will sell quite well in the liberal AND conservative political community, without your input?

Think about it. Talk it over with Karl.

But I expect to publish the eBook before Christmas. It will be a nice present for those who enjoy political intrigue.

Yours in Christ,

Bill Schmalfeldt

2 THE NATIONAL BLOGGERS CLUB AND THEIR SUPER PAC FRIENDS

(From an article co-authored by Matt Osborne, Alex Brent-Zawadzki and Bill Schmalfeldt with research assistance by Melissa Brewer. Originally published at Crooks and Liars, Sept. 12, 2012)

Ali Akbar, now President of the National Bloggers Club, is one of the conservative blogosphere's most infamous characters. He began his campaign of notoriety with a crime spree in 2006, blazing a six-year trail of fraud. That's him up there, in the mug shots. Akbar's story is as improbable as the Tea Party movement itself, and a lesson on the privileges of power in the age of Citizens United. How did a petty crook rise to these heights in such a short time? Why does he enjoy such influential connections today?

We ask these questions because we see an emerging bipartisan consensus that Akbar's National Bloggers Club (NBC) is entirely notional. Akbar has never applied to the IRS for 501(c)3 status -- despite having claimed as much on the NBC Facebook page. While the NBC requires an unusual amount of personal information from donors, they do not offer those donors an EIN (Employer ID Number) to make their contributions tax deductible.

An EIN is provided upon application for nonprofit status, and should be available if the National Bloggers Club has applied. It is an easy online process. Yet we have been unable to locate an EIN in any database, and inquiries by both liberal and conservative bloggers have been met with silence. When journalist Bill Schmalfeldt contacted the Internal Revenue Service, he was informed that no EIN existed in their database for a National Bloggers Club.

This would be less distressing if Akbar didn't have a long history of covering up his tracks and minimizing his criminal past. In 2006, he stole items from a woman's home; he later broke into a vehicle, stole a debit card, and withdrew money from the victim's account, earning a felony conviction. Yet this record did not keep Akbar out of Republican politics.

Barely a year later, Akbar was accused of discussing election fraud tactics. The accuser, Joey A. Dauben, was a former colleague. In coverage of the controversy, Akbar was frequently and mistakenly identified as a John McCain campaign staffer due to his involvement in Bloggers for McCain, a "cooperating" website independent from the campaign itself. Akbar also caught flak for "scrubbing the web" to cover the tracks of Michael Meissner, a former police chief who was charged with posing as a woman and soliciting photos of under-aged boys.

In April 2008, Akbar pleaded guilty to the debit card fraud and was sentenced to four years probation and restitution of the stolen money. His probation ended in May of this year. In the meantime, Akbar has built quite a blog empire for himself -- and runs it from his mother's house.

By 2008 Akbar had linked up with Eric Odom's Don't Go movement. They likely met up when Akbar's firm, Republic Modern, designed the old website of Sam Adams Alliance, for which Odom was the new media director. When Odom started American Liberty Alliance (ALA), a tea party website that was mainly in the business of monetizing other Tea Party sites with ads, he brought Akbar along with him. Starting off as ALA's Technology Consultant, Akbar would eventually became Chairman of ALA's Board, spending much of his time collecting non-deductible donations.

Yes, despite claiming to be in the application process for 501(c) 4 status in August 2009, ALA eventually was embarrassed into posting the following caveat on their website (though not their donation page): "The American Liberty Alliance is not a 501c3, 501c4 or a PAC. We are not registered as a non-profit and we do not raise funds as such." Yet they incorporated under the name "American Liberty Alliance - A Non-Profit Corporation."

The most excoriating examination of the ALA came from Erick Erickson, who reported that ALA had eventually been rolled up into an Eric Odom PAC:

For a number of months I have had more than my share of phone calls from conservative donors, bloggers, activists, campaigns, and others wishing someone would speak out. Several tried pushing this story into the mainstream media, but we all know what would happen there ? we'd turn people into martyrs who shouldn't be.

At best this conduct looks like ignorance of the complex bureaucracy and regulations surrounding the FEC. At its worst, it looks like… well, you decide. I'm sure even more will come out now that I'm willing to speak up and it does not look like a case of simple ignorance. If it were an isolated incident it'd be one thing, but it is a pattern.

Indeed, the pattern begins with a profitable deception. Although ALA was registered as a non-profit in Nevada, as far as we can determine they never actually applied for non-profit status with the IRS, despite always claiming they were "in the process" of doing so. The pattern repeats with NBC, which incorporated in Texas as a non-profit, and has collected donations as a non-profit, without ever applying for legal non-profit designation. (The NBC has scrubbed 501(c)3 language from its donations page at Rally.org.)

Our attempts to reach the law firm listed as the NBC's registered agent have been rebuffed. (Update: the address appears to be a "virtual" office.)

These dubious credentials in the new Tea Party movement propelled Akbar into the upper echelons of conservative organizing, where he has apparently met Karl Rove.

Yet Akbar seems to have done remarkably little real work during his ascension. Take the NBC's website, for example, which contains no content -- just a redirect to the group's Facebook page.

There, you will find grassroots conservatives wondering how to join, and why the donation practices are so intrusive:

Like many of Akbar's websites, content doesn't seem to be key. For example, despite supposedly representing a robust movement, Akbar's Tea Party Brew.com has surprisingly few posts. Bill Murphy, now the Social Media Director for the Romney campaign, wrote the final post at that site in February. By then, he had been Akbar's venture partner since 2009.

Murphy (right) was
Director of Strategic
Initiatives for American
Liberty Alliance, though
the position does not
appear on his LinkedIn
resume. Murphy was also
Akbar's partner in an
organization called Vice &
Victory, which put on the
BlogBash party at CPAC
in February. Akbar was
listed as the Host

Organizer and Murphy as the Event Coordinator.
BlogBash's director is usually identified as Devon
Wills, but many of NBC's announcements and press
releases offer contact information for "Bill Murphy at
director@blogbash.com." Yet the BlogBash website
doesn't even mention the NBC, which supposedly
organized the event.

When he appeared on the radio program of
conservative Larry Sinclair in March, Murphy also
identified himself as the Director of the NBC --
though that position also does not appear on his

resume. Whenever he has been asked about such omissions, Murphy has responded by further scrubbing his LinkedIn profile. Sinclair now calls foul on Akbar and Murphy's notional blogging club for using Andrew Breitbart's name to raise money for a scholarship fund -- again, while claiming 501(3)c status was "pending:"

In March 2012 we received an email which came from Bill Murphy and Ali Akbar from BlogBash.org and Vice and Victory email addresses announcing the creation of an Andrew Breitbart Scholarship Fund. After receiving the email and because of our own personal encounters with Andrew Sinclair News decided we would do a feature story on the Scholarship fund. In preparing the story we sent an email to Joel Pollak who was the primary Breitbart.com principle since the untimely death of Andrew early the morning of March 1, 2012. In the email to Mr. Pollak we asked if Pollak would be interested in going on Through the Mirror w/Larry Sinclair to talk about the recently established Breitbart Scholarship Fund. **Pollak responded almost immediately by telling us he knew nothing of any such fund; that anyone using**

Andrews name along with any such fund was doing so without authorization and Pollak even went to the point of saying that any such organization was in his opinion a scam.
(Emphasis added)

Aside from Michelle Malkin, nobody knows who is on the board of the NBC, or how they were selected. NBC won't even say whether they have any bylaws, and has never applied for non-profit status. If the NBC was an ACORN office, Malkin would denounce it as a criminal organization. Instead, she is Akbar's public ally and defender.

These inconsistencies had already drawn criticism from conservatives when we began reporting on them. First was Paul Lemmen, a convicted con artist working out his redemption in his blog, "An Ex Con's View." As the details of Akbar's criminal record appeared on the website Breitbart Unmasked in May and June, Lemmen expressed disdain for the fact that "the other side" had been the one to reveal Akbar's criminal past. Citing the NBC's disturbing lack of transparency and its behavior with donors, Lemmen called for transparency and accountability.

As a result of his outspoken blogging, Lemmen received the close attention of NBC "enforcer" and Andrew Breitbart protégé Lee Stranahan amid a series of attack posts by other bloggers. Lemmen fell silent for a while, reemerging later to write on more general topics. Today, he is a member of North American Conservative Bloggers United (NACBU), a new association of conservative indie bloggers opposed to the NBC and its opaque operations. In supporting Lemmen, David West called out Akbar for elitism:

See, Ali Akbar was the 'technical guru' for a while behind the Don't Go Movement which I was a part of as Northwest Regional Coordinator. I, however, was ignored back then by Mr Ackbar. When he formed the NBC, I was ignored as well.

The NBC billed itself in part as an organization that could give bloggers desperately-needed press credentials. Those who have received credentials are unable to activate them as instructed. The NBC does not explain how to receive a credential, or even describe any standards for applicants. NACBU organizer "Impolite Canadian" just wanted to

webcast an event; after being rebuffed in all
attempts to learn more about how to obtain the
privileges of membership, the pseudonymous
blogger concluded that NBC was simply a club of
Akbar's friends:

It's like they all of a sudden became part of the
"elites", encouraging and defending the
"mastermind", but when asked how does one join
this "elite" club, you get the "I dunno man, it just
happened, u know?".

There are only 340 "likes" on the NBC Facebook
page at the time of this writing -- far fewer than one
would expect for a popular netroots organization.
Ladd Ehlinger, Jr., aka FilmLadd, questioned
whether the NBC was even a real organization:

**Screw Ali's political connections. You
love him? Want to blacklist me? Be my
guest. Won't be the first time that's
happened. Been happening for two years
now anyway. It's the sort of thing I think
Ali likes to do to people who get
crosswise with him - trash them, prevent
them from getting work, and so on. I**

**could regale you with first-hand stories
I've heard, but this post is already too
goddamn long.**

Akbar did not prevent Ladd from getting work. In
fact, Ehlinger received a plum new gig from
Washington lobbyist Dan Backer of DB Capitol
Strategies. He serves as Treasurer for many well-
known PACs, including the Conservative Action
Fund, which has already given Akbar's "Vice &
Victory Fund" over $44,000 in 2012. Backer is also
Treasurer for Stop This Insanity Inc PAC, which
recently signed Ehlinger to a complex $10,000
contract. Ehlinger hasn't spoken out on the subject

of Ali Akbar ever since.
(CORRECTION: see
below)

Backer (right) is the
attorney who created
"hybrid Super PACs"
through his Carey v. FEC
lawsuit in 2011. As part of
his contract, Ehlinger

agreed to be classified as an employee and then kick back $1,500 to Stop This Insanity Inc PAC, creating an opportunity to challenge federal limits on employee PAC contributions. Backer also wants to lift limits on contributions to federal candidates. True freedom, Backer argues, is American billionaires donating more hard political money every year than an average American family makes.

Dan Backer's other PAC products include Todd Cefaratti, who became infamous for fleecing PAC donors and using his for-profit JoinTheTeaParty.us website as a lead generator for spam. Cefaratti was found out by activists at Free Republic, who quickly discovered that his real estate sales lead business was named Glengary Inc. Despite grassroots revulsion at this character from a David Mamet play, Cefaratti spoke at CPAC in February. He and his Glengary LLC are also party to Dan Backer's FEC suit with Ehlinger. Stop This Insanity Inc. runs another one of Cefaratti's websites, TheTeaParty.net.

The "made men" of the Inner Party are never held accountable. Their revolution has been monetized: shirts, buttons, email addresses, and page views turn dedicated activists into revenue streams for "producers." Meanwhile, these same "producers" also get paid by billionaires and PAC lawyers who benefit from stoking the grassroots fires on behalf of their corporate agenda. It's a great job if you can get it. No wonder Akbar likes to throw big, exclusive parties at CPAC and the Republican National Convention.

In order to make the BlogBash party an instant institution this year, Akbar and Murphy took money from a host of the usual suspects in Astroturf politics, including Americans For Prosperity, FreedomWorks, and the vote-suppressing True The Vote organization. Billionaire and mega-donor Foster Friess also helped throw Akbar's party at CPAC, then cracked a terrible joke about aspirin as a form of birth control: "You know, back in my days, they used Bayer Aspirin for contraception. The gals put it between their knees, and it wasn't that costly." Friess has vowed to spend a large chunk of his fortune through Karl Rove's American Crossroads this year.

We believe the National Bloggers Club encapsulates a problem common to Tea Party organizing since February 2009. As with Mark Meckler, the multilevel marketing billionaire who organized Tea Party Patriots, we see a disturbing pattern of grift in the National Bloggers Club. Sincere Americans have been organized to prevent corporate regulation and billionaire tax hikes; the organizers fleece them while also accepting money from representatives of these same corporations and billionaires.

This charade may be close to an end, however. Larry Sinclair has presented the National Bloggers Club with a demand they publish the following:

The names of every National Bloggers Club Board member including the date each became associated with the NBC

A complete financial report showing the amounts of all monies paid to in contributions; services; or sponsorships made to NBC or BlogBash.

A Complete financial reporting of all funds paid out by NBC or BlogBash including the names of those receiving said payments and the reasons for each.

A complete financial accounting of all funds paid out by NBC/Blogbash including an accounting of what the payments were for and if they were made for the personal benefit of Ali Akbar or any other member of the NBC Board.

A complete accounting of all contributions made to the Breitbart Scholarship Fund as well as an accounting of all disbursements of said funds as well as the name of the financial institution(s) where contributions are on deposit.

A statement as to Bill Murphy's position with NBC and BlogBash; whether Murphy has been involved in any NBC/BlogBash activities and or promotions since becoming Mitt Romney for President Social Media Director?

The IRS 501(c)(3) documents confirming the below stated claim by NBC:

"National Bloggers Club is a new 501(c)(3) founded by top new media operatives, bloggers and journalists as a loose association of bloggers who are for

**free enterprise and limited government
and to advocate on bloggers behalf."**

In the spirit of nonpartisan opposition to criminal
misbehavior and opaque political activity, we join
these conservative voices in calling for
accountability. Akbar has been dishonest about his
criminal record. His organization has been
dishonest about its non-profit status. The NBC did
not ask Breitbart's family before asking for
donations in his name. Their associations with
powerful figures in the world of campaign finance
have not been able to fully silence grassroots
opposition to their questionable practices:

These aren't unfair questions. They are very simple,
basic questions spoken without malice or any
agenda save that of telling the truth. And has
already been noted, the truth has no agenda. It's
just the truth.

Conservative bloggers are asking for simple
transparency -- and being refused. Liberal bloggers
meet only scorn and harassment for asking the
same legitimate questions. We believe it is time for
"real" journalists to consider this information, as no

mere blogger of any political persuasion will ever glean answers from the National Bloggers Club or their Super PAC friends. They are apparently a law unto themselves.

 Ali A. Akbar @ali   21h
Breaking: you're not a real journalist if "I'm not going to talk about any of it" is a sign of guilt or THE story.
Expand

C

ORRECTION: Advised via Twitter that Ladd Ehlinger had recently denounced Ali Akbar on Twitter, we include the following items for your consideration:

@xcitizen10 @brooksbayne When I came out against Ali, it was after extended 1st hand evidence. Not hearsay, not Twitter snark. 1st hand.

— Film Ladd (@FilmLadd) September 6, 2012

@xcitizen10 @brooksbayne Let's do a reality check on that. Ever got a link from either's blog? (er, Ali doesn't actually blog, but...)

— Film Ladd (@FilmLadd) September 7, 2012

@brooksbayne @xcitizen10 1st, I can agree to disagree w/others in regards to Lee or Ali w/out lining 'em up in front of Twitter firing squad

— Film Ladd (@FilmLadd) September 6, 2012

@thecypressgang @aaronworthing @brooksbayne 2nd, reasonable people can disagree over Ali being a p.o.s. Con-men are good at confusing folks.

— Film Ladd (@FilmLadd) September 6, 2012

Life was not easy for young **Ali Akbar.** Son of a single mother. Two younger brothers at home. At first glance, this is easily a story that looks like it will have an unhappy ending.

So, how does young Akbar go from being convicted for stealing from a woman, breaking into a van, stealing and using a debit card; to becoming a top operative in the Young Republican Party movement, all in the span of slightly more than five years?

Working with another writer at the blog **"Breitbart Unmasked"** (named after the deceased conservative muckraker Andrew Breitbart who died on March 1, 2012), the author discovered that Ali Akbar was a key player in the creation of an organization called **"The National Bloggers Club, Inc."**, which -- at that time -- advertised itself as a 501(c)(3) organization, meaning if you donated money to them, you could file a tax deduction. The organization was ostensibly created to provide legal funds for Aaron Walker, a lawyer who claimed he was under attack by Brett Kimberlin, the convicted **"Speedway Bomber"** whose series of bombings in the late 70s injured one person so severely, he used it as a reason to take his own life years later. Since being released from jail, Kimberlin has seemingly turned his interests toward progressive causes. Walker and other right wing bloggers -- led at the time by

Breitbart -- launched a campaign against Kimberlin.

Ali Akbar, as founder and CEO of an agency called **Vice and Victory**, decided to form the National Bloggers Club to raise money to aid in Walker's defense against Kimberlin.

The author tried to contact Akbar as he had done many times in his career to ask him to provide some evidence that his 501(c)(3) was legitimate. As seen in the first chapter, the author was spurned in his attempt to get information.

One way to get an investigative journalist really, really interested in learning more about you? Refuse a simple request for publicly-available information.

With a colleague at the **"Breitbart Unmasked"** blog, the author discovered that Mr. Akbar had some secrets he didn't seem to want his followers to know about.

For one, there was that matter of a month long theft spree in November 2006, in which Mr. Akbar was accused of stealing five MP3 players, 20 CDs, three camcorders, two DVD players, one back massager, one clock, four shirts, two belts and a piece of luggage from a person in Tarrant

County, Texas. (Indictment # 1052509)

Then, there was the matter of breaking into a van on December 5, 2006, with the intent to commit theft. (Tarrant County Case #1080568)

Then, we have the slight problem of Mr. Akbar's attempt to fraudulently use a debit card he allegedly stole during his alleged break in of the alleged van. (Tarrant County Case #1080448)

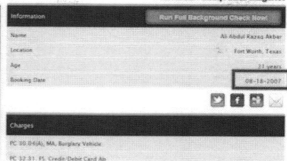

Ali Abdul Razaq Akbar Mugshot

Information — Run Full Background Check Now!

Name	Ali Abdul Razaq Akbar
Location	Fort Worth, Texas
Age	21 years
Booking Date	08-18-2007

Charges

PC 30.04(A), MA, Burglary Vehicle

PC 32.31, FS, Credit/Debit Card Ab

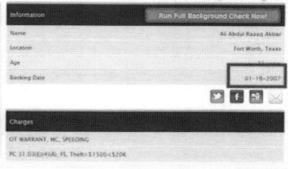

Ali Abdul Razaq Akbar Mugshot

Information — Run Full Background Check Now!

Name	Ali Abdul Razaq Akbar
Location	Fort Worth, Texas
Age	
Booking Date	01-16-2007

Charges

OT WARRANT, MC, SPEEDING

PC 31.03(E)(4)(A), FS, Theft>$1500<$20K

NAME ALI AKBAR	OFFENSE CREDIT/DEBIT CARD ABUSE
ADDRESS ▮▮▮▮▮▮▮▮ PLACE	DATE 12/5/2006
FORT WORTH TX 76137	I.P. RUSSELL HUFFMAN
RACE B SEX M AGE 21 ▮▮▮▮	
CASE NO. 1080448 DATE FILED 8/22/2007	AGENCY Fort Worth PD
CID NO. 0699828	OFFENSE NO. 06142175
	COURT 213th District Court

INDICTMENT NO. 1080448 D

IN THE NAME AND BY AUTHORITY OF THE STATE OF TEXAS:

THE GRAND JURORS OF TARRANT COUNTY, TEXAS,

duly elected, tried, empaneled, sworn, and charged to inquire of offenses committed in Tarrant County, in the State of Texas, upon their oaths do present in and to the

CRIMINAL DISTRICT COURT NO. 4

of said County that ALI AKBAR, hereinafter called Defendant, in the County of Tarrant and State aforesaid, on or about the 5th day of December 2006, did

WITH THE INTENT TO FRAUDULENTLY OBTAIN A BENEFIT, PRESENT OR USE A DEBIT CARD, TO-WIT: A WELLS FARGO DEBIT CARD WITH THE KNOWLEDGE THAT SAID CARD HAD NOT BEEN ISSUED TO THE SAID DEFENDANT, AND WITH THE KNOWLEDGE THAT SAID CARD WAS NOT USED WITH THE EFFECTIVE CONSENT OF RUSSELL HUFFMAN, THE CARDHOLDER,

ALI AKBAR	§	TARRANT COUNTY, TEXAS

UNADJUDICATED JUDGMENT ON PLEA OF GUILTY OR NOLO CONTENDERE AND SUSPENDING IMPOSITION OF SENTENCE

Judge Presiding	: HON. LOUIS E. STURNS	Date of Judgment	: APRIL 25, 2008
Attorney for State District Attorney	: TIM CURRY	Assistant District Attorney	: CHRISTY JACK
Attorney for Defendant	: HOWARD ROSENSTEIN	Charging Instrument: INDICTMENT	
Offense Date	Offense		
DECEMBER 5, 2006	DEBIT CARD ABUSE		
Degree	Count	Plea	
STATE JAIL	ONE	GUILTY	
Findings on Deadly Weapon	: NONE		
Plea to Enhancement Paragraph(s)	: NONE		
Plea to Habitual Paragraph(s)	: NONE		
Findings on Enhancement/ Habitual Paragraph(s)	: NONE		
Punishment	: DEFERRED	Date to Commence	: APRIL 25, 2008
Probationary Term	: FOUR (4) YEARS		
Fine Not Suspended	: $400.00 FOUR HUNDRED DOLLARS AND ZERO CENTS		
	: FINE IN THE AMOUNT OF $400.00 AND COURT COSTS IN THE AMOUNT OF $276.00, PAYABLE TO AND THROUGH THE DISTRICT CLERK OF TARRANT COUNTY, TEXAS		

On this day, set forth above, this cause came for trial and came the State of Texas, by its above-named attorney, and the Defendant appeared in person and by the above-named attorney for the Defendant, or, where a Defendant is not represented by counsel, that the Defendant knowingly, intelligently, and voluntarily waived the right to representation by counsel; and announced ready for trial, the Defendant having been heretofore arraigned, or having waived arraignment in open court, and having agreed that the testimony may be stipulated in this cause and the Defendant, his counsel, and the State's attorney having agreed in writing in open court to waive a jury in the trial of this cause and to submit this cause to the Court, and the Court having agreed to the same, the said attorney for the State read the instrument charging the offense as shown or the reading of the charging instrument having been waived by Defendant, the Defendant entered his plea as shown above thereto, and it appearing to the Court that the Defendant is mentally competent and the plea is free and voluntary, and the Court having duly admonished the Defendant as to the consequences of such plea, including the range of punishment attached to the offense and the fact that any recommendation of the prosecuting attorney as to punishment is not binding on the Court, and the Defendant further having affirmatively stated awareness of the consequences of such plea and acknowledged to not having been misled or harmed by the admonishment of the Court, yet the Defendant persisted in entering such plea, said plea is by the Court received and now entered of record upon the minutes of the Court as the plea herein of said Defendant. The Court after receiving the plea shown and hearing the evidence, finds that it substantiates the Defendant's guilt and that further proceedings should be deferred without entering an adjudication of guilt and that Defendant should be placed on probation on reasonable terms and conditions as the Court may require.

The State of Texas do have and recover of the said Defendant all costs in this prosecution expended including any fine shown above for which let execution issue. And it is further ORDERED by the Court that the imposition of sentence of the judgment of conviction herein shall be suspended during the good behavior of the Defendant and that the Defendant be placed on probation during the period of time, fixed by the Court, under the conditions to be determined by the Court, as provided by law. However, when it is shown above that a fine applicable to the offense committed has been imposed by the Court and not suspended, then it is ORDERED that Defendant pay such fine and all costs in this prosecution expended and that Defendant be placed on probation during the period of time fixed by the Court, under the conditions to be determined by the Court, as provided by law.

IT IS THEREFORE CONSIDERED by the Court that the evidence substantiates the Defendant's guilt and that further proceedings should be Deferred without entering an adjudication of guilt, and that Defendant be placed on probation during the period of time prescribed by the Court on such reasonable terms and conditions as the Court may require in accordance with law.

Akbar took a plea bargain that deferred adjudication, providing he kept his nose clean for four years.

When the author and his colleague went public with their charges and documentation, Akbar offered an **explanation to his followers on Facebook** which reads, in part:

"One night, a friend asked to be taken to work, but first he wanted to stop by the ATM. I was "the guy with the car" so after dropping of my other friends, I rushed him to the ATM. He was already late to work and he had become irritated. He had a bad temper so my goal was to simply keep the situation calm and under control. He kept slicing the card through, typed in his PIN, but for whatever reason he couldn't get funds out. On the drive to drop him off he explained to me that it was not his card. It belonged to his previous roommate and he said the person owed him money. Shame and horror fell over me -- and it still does."

Odd. No mention of any of that in the charging documents, for which Akbar took a guilty plea in April 2008, receiving a four year suspended sentence and a $400 fine.

With that episode behind him, apparently a change of scenery was in order for young Mr. Akbar.

3 WHAT TO DO, WHAT TO DO?

Before the plea agreement was signed in April 2008, Akbar had a chance to get involved in his first **political** scandal, according to the website **Libertarian Republican.** The website reported that Akbar was heard discussing ways to steal an election.

Statement from one of the two witnesses Joey Dauben of ***South Dallas****:*

*I sat in on a meeting in my downtown Dallas office and heard an ecampaign staffer with the **John McCain campaign** – Ali A. Akbar – openly discuss ways to manipulate, rig and otherwise "take" an election*

Akbar's position with the McCain Campaign:

Akbar is the "E-Campaign Coordinator" for the John

McCain for President Campaign. He is listed on "Bloggers for McCain" as one of the 5 Authors. There's also a report that he's the graphics designer, or at least a contributing designer for McCain's main campaign website. In addition, he is a campaign spokesperson for the Texas McCain Campaign.

The editor of The Liberal Grouch, who asked that his name not be used in this series of stories, did not know what the terms of Akbar's probation were. But at some point he moseyed on down to Ellis County, Texas where he did some **work for a news website** called the Ellis County Observer.

(A former cop named Michael) Meissner worked with an Ali Akbar, who was on probation for credit card abuse and theft, to suppress online records of his misdeeds. Akbar was an executive editor and webmaster at the Observer, *but was accused by **proprietor (Joe) Dauben of endorsing voter fraud tactics.** (See above!) But Akbar helped Dauben determine via IP address tracing certain posts that on the* Observer *that he says were made by his arch-enemy (fellow cop John) Hoskins. And even though Dauben is alleged to be in league with Meissner, **he published some pretty damning stuff about him at the Press**.*

Politics = strange bedfellows. Who are these other players? From the same story.

*There was a **widely reported story last week about the arrest of a "former police chief" named Michael Meissner** who is charged with posing as a woman and soliciting nude photos from underage boys. He's actually a **gypsy cop** who **moved from town to town**, allegedly leaving perhaps hundreds of victims in his wake.*

(snip)

*Dauben is better known as **Joey Dauben**, and was the young publisher I'd learned about on YouTube. He isn't actually wanted in conjunction with the molestation charges, but on **charges related to an alleged scheme to defame police officers involved in the Meissner investigation** — specifically, misuse of official information; obstruction or retaliation; and engaging in organized criminal activity.*

Charges were eventually dropped against Meissner and Dauben, although Dauben was later indicted in Feb. 2012 for fraudulent use of identifying information **while in the hoosegow facing four counts of sexual abuse of a child**.

No money, no visible means of support. What's a young Republican to do?

In 2008, before moving to Georgia, Akbar was featured in a **Dallas Morning News** story.

Hip Hop Republicans

comments (0)

By Emily Ramshaw/Reporter
eramshaw@...
7:17 pm on September 2, 2008 | Permalink

There's no denying it, Ali Akbar says. When you're half black and half Arab and at the Republican National Convention, "you stand out like a sore thumb."

But this 22-year-old Texan and other young African Americans who identify themselves as "Hip Hop Republicans" are hoping to put their stamp on the party.

Mr. Akbar, who was born to a single mom in Dallas, said it would've been easy for him to just assume he was a Democrat — something he says many black Americans do.

"I thought I was a Democrat," he said. "I think all African Americans do at some point."

But on his debate team at Keller's Foster Ridge High School, his debate coach inspired him to really read economic theory. Mr. Akbar said he quickly became convinced that fiscal responsibility — and in particular, the tax cuts supported by the Republican Party, would improve prosperity for urban minorities.

It's a theory that's being offered to young black voters through a web forum for black Republican bloggers called Hip Hop Republican.

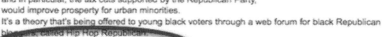

Mr. Akbar, a University of North Texas student who is about to trasfer to Georgia Southern University, is spending this week volunteering on the convention's floor operations team. He also operates several political Web sites.

"I believe there's something better for the black community that just assuming you're a Democrat," he said.

Mr. Akbar, a University of North Texas student who is about to trasfer to Georgia Southern University, is spending this week volunteering on the convention's floor operations team. He also operates several political Web sites.

A check with the registrar at the University of North
Texas showed that Akbar did, in fact, attend the
university. For one semester. Three months. In 2005. But
yes, he did move to Georgia. We are waiting on word as
to whether or not he actually enrolled at Georgia
Southern.

You have contacted the right people. It appears that Ali Akbar was enrolled from August to December of 2005 for the Fall semester. If you
have any other questions, feel free to contact us.

Anna J.
Registrar's Office
(940) 565-2113
registrar@unt.edu

But why move to Georgia?

In the author's blog at the time, he offered this
explanation.

*It is now May 2008. Prominent Georgia conservative
blogger, "The Peach Pundit" is whining about the lack
of decent candidates to run against incumbent
Democratic congressman John Barrow. In the blog's
comment section, Akbar invites "the Peach Pundit" to
meet with Georgia congressional candidate Ray
McKinney.*

*Now, one can wonder how young Akbar became
acquainted with Mr. McKinney. It would seem that a hot,
young Republican on probation would cross paths with a*

Georgia conservative… when that Georgia conservative waves some money in his face during the Texas Straw Poll in Fort Worth in late 2007.

According to Wikipedia, McKinney (who did not return e-mails asking for comment for this story) won the Texas Straw Poll, surprising -- shocking, in fact -- the establishment candidates. This fame did not carry over to a win in the congressional primary, so Akbar put aside his support for McKinney for the time being and began working for Tea Party candidate Rob Hoffman in the special election in the New York 23rd Congressional District.

But where was he getting all the money to travel the nation like this? He wasn't flush with cash. In fact, he was evicted from his new home in Savannah, Georgia, for non-payment of rent in 2010.

Oddly enough, here's where the young survivor's career

begins to skyrocket.

Before his eviction in 2010, in October 2009 Akbar had the financial ability to travel to upstate New York to work for the Tea Party candidate in the special election in the New York 23rd district. Owens won that election handily. Akbar's third campaign, Akbar's third losing candidate.

With that disappointment behind him, Akbar was right back to work with McKinney on his second attempt to win the GOP nomination for that congressional district in Georgia. McKinney gets the nomination. But McKinney's opponent alleged wrongdoing.

After his opponent didn't even show up for a debate in the 2010 GOP Congressional Primary in Georgia's 12th congressional district, candidate Carl Smith had the podium to himself. He addressed the empty podium and asked a series of questions that went unanswered.

After the "debate," Smith handed out flyers alleging that his opponent, Ray McKinney, was illegally collaborating with a political action committee known as the One Nation PAC. Specifically, that McKinney's campaign manager, a young computer whiz named Ali A. Akbar, was on the board of that PAC and that the campaign was using the same mailing service as the PAC.

McKinney, who won the primary but lost the general election to the Democratic incumbent, called the allegations nonsense. For his part, Akbar says he wasn't the campaign manager for McKinney, he severed all ties with One Nation PAC and there were no improprieties.

However, documents revealed in a **CNN iReport** recently show Akbar may have to clarify those remarks.

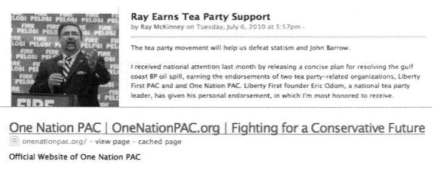

Ray Earns Tea Party Support
by Ray McKinney on Tuesday, July 6, 2010 at 5:57pm ·

The tea party movement will help us defeat statism and John Barrow.

I received national attention last month by releasing a concise plan for resolving the gulf coast BP oil spill, earning the endorsements of two tea party–related organizations, Liberty First PAC and and One Nation PAC. Liberty First founder Eric Odom, a national tea party leader, has given his personal endorsement, in which I'm most honored to receive.

One Nation PAC | OneNationPAC.org | Fighting for a Conservative Future
onenationpac.org/ – view page – cached page
Official Website of One Nation PAC

All posts about this link   ☐ Show influential only (1)

kellyseustis Kelly S. Eustis
RT @OneNationPAC RT @Ali Please sign up for @OneNationPAC :: http://onenationpac.org ... love yo #politics #sgp
10/28/2009 ↩ Reply ⇄ Retweet ☆ Favorite

onenationpac One Nation PAC
RT @Ali Please sign up for @OneNationPAC :: http://onenationpac.org ... love your country. #tcot #n
10/28/2009 ↩ Reply ⇄ Retweet ☆ Favorite

ali Ali A. Akbar Highly Influential
Please sign up for @OneNationPAC :: http://onenationpac.org ... love your country.
10/28/200 ↩ Reply ⇄ Retweet ☆ Favorite

12th District runoff: Smith accuses McKinney of coordination with a PAC

Smith accuses fellow Republican McKinney of coordination with a PAC

Posted: July 26, 2010 - 12:18am | Updated: July 26, 2010 - 8:05am

savannahnow.

ATLANTA - Carl Smith faced Raymond McKinney's empty lectern Sunday evening during a statewide televised debate of the Republicans in the runoff for the nomination to the 12th congressional district. But the mud flew after the program.

Smith accused McKinney of violating federal election law by coordinating with a political-action committee based in California regarding an attack mailer delivered across the district the weekend before Tuesday's primary.

The two Republicans came in first and second place Tuesday, landing in the Aug. 10 runoff for the chance to face Rep. John Barrow, D-Ga., in November.

McKinney's spokesman said Friday that the candidate had a schedule conflict that didn't allow a 10-hour roundtrip to the Atlanta studios of Georgia Public Broadcasting where the Atlanta Press Club hosts its forums.

Smith, though, had the 20-minute segment to himself to respond to questions from a panel of reporters and even to "question" the absent McKinney. He asked McKinney's empty lectern about a boast at the beginning of the campaign that he had $100,000 in contributions which turned out to be money McKinney poured into the kitty from his personal coffers.

"I just want to ask Mr. McKinney why he felt he couldn't trust the voters with that information," Smith said, adding that it cast a shadow of mistrust.

But it was after the forum that he distributed documents accusing improper coordination between McKinney's campaign and the One Nation PAC. The documents note that McKinney supporter Ali A. Akbar served on the One Nation board and that the pac and the campaign used the same mailing company.

The documents list Akbar as McKinney's campaign manager, but Akbar said the campaign operates without one and that he is just a volunteer. He also said he resigned from the honorary board position in April and never had any say in the pac's activities.

"Neither the McKinney campaign nor I had any coordination with the One Nation PAC," Akbar said when reached by phone. "I'm not paid by the McKinney campaign. ... I'm helping Ray because he's a friend."

Also in the papers is what appears to be a copy of an e-mail from Akbar from before the One Nation mailer's delivery to GOP households across the district. In the e-mail, Akbar mentions One Nation as one of several organizations that would be helpful to McKinney.

Smith notes that the One Nation mailer attacked him for the same things McKinney has blasted him for, such as having supported Democrats in past elections, being fired from his jobs as firefighter and allegedly breaking a federal law prohibiting federally funded government officials from running for partisan political positions. The similarity, Smith said, is more evidence of coordination, but other candidates in the primary raised most of the same issues.

"Somebody needs to find out if they've been violating election laws," Smith said of McKinney.

Akbar's **March 2011 Technorati profile** indicates his membership on the One Nation PAC without any mention of his work for McKinney, who Akbar seems to have dropped like a hot rock when McKinney lost in the 2010 general election.

These documents, taken with the already established fact that Ali **lied** to his current crop of supporters about his felony convictions in 2008, the established fact that he **lied** about the 501(c)(3) status of his "National Bloggers Club," and **several other prevarications and non-truth-tellings**, combined with his unwillingness to directly answer any questions about his past life asked by a non-supporter and the fact that Karl Rove (who Ali admitted on a widely circulated **YouTube video** as being someone he had closely worked with) **claimed intellectual property rights over an image of Ali**, wearing an Obama mask and waving $20 bills (the flash shadows in the picture indicate it was taken from a position in front of, below and very close to Ali) raises even more questions about the startling, meteoric rise of this ex-con with no college education, no visible means of support, no training, no prospects, and nothing to indicate how he became one of the brightest stars in the Young Republican constellation without the help of...*someone.*

If either Mr. Akbar or Mr. Rove would deign to answer direct questions, it would be much easier to get to the bottom of this growing potential scandal. However both have ignored numerous requests for comment leaving themselves open to the rampant speculation and vicious "tongue-wagging" for which the "inside the Beltway" pundits are so famous.

McKinney gets his butt handed to him by the incumbent. Akbar drops McKinney like he's hot. But still, with no place to live, with no visible means of support, what does an ex-con with political ambitions do?

Perhaps... find a sugar daddy?

4 MAKING CONNECTIONS

Ali Akbar. You're an ex-con with no education. You've had some success ingratiating yourself into the regional tea party scene with your work for two losing candidates. But now, you have no home, you have no job, you have no money. What do you do? A good way to start? You hook up with the National Tea Party scene. You catch the eye of Tea Party blogger R. Stacy McCain.

Conservatives Launch NotMittRomney.com

Posted on | November 7, 2011 | 38 Comments and 6 Reactions

New Media genius Ali Akbar strikes again with NotMittRomney.com, a petition endorsed by many familiar names — including John Hawkins and Pamela Geller — and gets a write-up from Zeke Miller at Business Insider:

> A coalition of conservatives have launched a campaign against Republican front-runner Mitt Romney's candidacy to prevent him from becoming the GOP nominee next year. The group's website, NotMittRomney.com, already features a web ad against the former Massachusetts governor — and they plan more "aggressive" steps in the coming months. ...

Read the whole thing. Here's their first 30-second video:

Here's their press release:

Then, somehow, from someone, somewhere, you get the money to fund a wide assortment of new ventures... including the Vice and Victory agency.

Your organization works to support the losing candidate in the College Republican National Committee race. (Another campaign, another losing candidate.)

Yet, despite a record of failure and felony, you're in the big time.

Your attempts to help bloggers with their legal fees in their fight against Brett has caught the attention of other bloggers who do what your donors, your friends, your supporters all failed to do. They look into the background of Ali A. Akbar.

They ask questions. Uncomfortable questions. If you are Ali Akbar, you deal with this by closing your eyes real tight, covering your ears, and pretend that none of this is happening.

Or, you tweet out insults and lies to your supporters in the hopes that they are stupid enough to believe you, thereby discrediting those who would dare question the motives of one so noble, one so pure.

Notorious right wing blogger Larry Sinclair was one such supporter in the early days. Say what you will about Larry, the individual who continues to maintain that he did cocaine with and provided "oral services" for a young Illinois state senator named Barack Obama. But when word of Akbar's felonious past was made public, Sinclair joined other conservative bloggers in condemning The National Bloggers Club and Akbar.

Akbar's response was to send out tweets reminding folks why Sinclair was notorious.

Ali A. Akbar @ali   12m
LOL. Word association: Cocaine, 27 year long criminal record, National Press Club presser, oral sex, non-use of spell check. You know!
Expand

Mr. Aye Dee @MrAyeDee   14m
Coke and head in the back of a limo? Lol RT @ali: So since Larry "Lisp" Sinclair has come after me with provable lies, should I run #Ali2024
🔁 Retweeted by Ali A. Akbar
Expand   ← Reply   ↻ Retweet   ★ Favorite

Ali A. Akbar @ali   15m
So since Larry "Lisp" Sinclair has come after me with provable lies, should I run for President? Worked for Obama. #Ali2024
Expand

But the thing about Larry Sinclair? He wears that notoriety like a badge of honor. Trying to "shame" Larry Sinclair is like telling your cat to stay off the shelf by the window. The cat looks at you like you're a moron and does what it wants to do, regardless of what you say.

In an article published on his Sinclair News website on November 12, 2012, Sinclair asked one of the sponsors involved in the original "Blog Bash" party, from which Akbar used donations to create the National Bloggers Club, if that sponsor was aware of Akbar's background as a debit card fraudster. Akbar was still on probation when the first event was held during CPAC 2012 in February.

That sponsor was the **NAACPC**, the National Association for the Advancement of Conservative People of ALL Colors.

One of the sponsors listed on the Blog Bash web site of the BB at CPAC 2012, the NAACPC spoke with Sinclair News today. At the request of the NAACPC we have agreed to only publish the organizations name because they simply do not want to have this controversy adversely affect their other projects (which they say will not have any

Akbar, Blog Bash or National Blogger Club association. According to the NAACPC, they were contacted by Anita MonCrief (seems Anita may have been Akbar's best Independent Contracted employee for Blog Bash) and asked if they would sponsor Blog Bash at CPAC 2012. Mrs. MonCrief according to the NAACPC told them "Ali is in charge" but it was MonCrief who handled the agreement and who NAACPC worked with. The Blog Bash web site which lists NAACPC as a $750 Sponsoring Guest was actually given $1000.00 by NAACPC.

NAACPC was asked the following questions:

Q: Did anyone, Anita MonCrief or Ali Akbar ever disclose to NAACPC that Ali was on probation out of Texas for a credit/debit card fraud conviction before during or after your sponsorship of Blog Bash at CPAC 2012?

Answer: NO

Q: Do you believe NAACPC should have been told about Ali's probation and conviction at the time you were asked to sponsor Blog Bash?

Answer: Yes

Q: Would the NAACPC have agreed to be a sponsor of Blog Bash at CPAC 2012 had you known of Akbar's probation and conviction?

Answer: No

Q: Was the NAACPC ever told their sponsorship fee would be used to launch a National Bloggers Club or be used for any purpose other than Blog Bash Party?

Answer: No. We were told it was for Blog Bash. The only mention of National Bloggers Club was that as a sponsor we would receive National Blogger Club membership and ID's which we still have never received.

Q: What were you offered/promised by Mrs. MonCrief or Blog Bash for your sponsorship?

Answer: Our name and logo on the Blog Bash web site; Advanced access to the agenda; advanced access to the event; introduction to popular bloggers by Anita; one piece of paper inserted into the gift bags; promise to promote and have bloggers promote our site and events. Anita had told us we could pay $1000.00 instead of the $750.00 or $4000.00 and we would be provided the items which we wanted as a sponsor.

Q: Did the NAACPC receive what it was promised in exchange for its sponsorship?

Answer: No, we were promised that as a sponsor we would be introduced to and given access to the BB Bloggers list. When we asked for a copy of the Bloggers list & contact info we were told we had to have donated $10,000.00 or more to be given the Bloggers list. We were asked who we wanted to be introduced to and were told we would be introduced to those individuals by Anita. We tried to pass out fliers and info on our group and were told at the event we could not pass anything out. Our name and logo never was displayed as was promised, we were not allowed to distribute any information about us at the event.

Q: Who were you seeking to be introduced to and who were you promised an introduction to?

Answer: We asked to meet Foster Friess; Michelle Malkin; Pamela Geller; Hugh Hewitt; Andrew Breitbart (we had been introduced to Andrew earlier by Steve Bannon) Townhall; HotAir; RedState; and National Review. At the event we were told the introduction would not be able to take place but that we would be introduced at a later date and time and would emailed later. No such email was ever received and none of the promised introductions were ever made.

Q: Are you telling us that one of the benefits to NAACPC sponsorship was that NAACPC would be introduced to individuals and organizations by Anita and Ali?

Answer: Yes

Q: Who specifically was NAACPC promised an introduction to for sponsoring Blog Bash at CPAC 2012?

Answer: We were promised an introduction to Foster Friess and Michelle Malkin for sure.

Q: Do you remember if Michelle Malkin was in attendance at Blog Bash CPAC 2012 or at CPAC 2012:

Answer: Michelle Malkin was NOT at Blog Bash at CPAC 2012. As for her being at CPAC 2012 we can only say we did not see her.

Q: After being informed of the fact that Ali Akbar was on felony probation at the time he was receiving money for sponsoring Blog Bash, do you think NAACPC and the other sponsors should have been told this information upfront by Ali, Blog Bash or Mrs. MonCrief?

Answer: Absolutely. We have known Anita for a while and consider to be friends, we can only think that she did not disclose this information to us because she didn't know it at the time. That is the only reason we could think as to why Anita did not tell us.

Q: Do you think that not fully disclosing that Ali Akbar was on probation for a felony credit/debit card fraud conviction to Blog Bash sponsors hurts the conservative groups that depend on sponsors and supporters to survive?

Answer: Yes, how can anyone call for transparency and accountability when they refuse to be transparent themselves.

Q: Will the NAACPC agree to sponsor any future Blog Bash or Ali Akbar organizations in the future?

Answer: Not under the current circumstances.

Q: Would you consider requesting a refund from Blog Bash and Ali Akbar?

Answer: Yes

Q: Have you had any other association with Ali Akbar or Blog Bash since CPAC 2012.

Answer: We ran into Ali at Blog Bash Tampa where Ali introduced us to Devon Wills who Ali said was in charge of Blog Bash Tampa. Ali told us that he wanted to stage a Blog Bash event at an upcoming event we have scheduled early next year and asked us to work with Devon on the logistics.

This episode, however, brings attention to the hold Akbar seems to have over some in the Conservative Community. No sooner had Sinclair published the responses from the NAACPC, their Chief Operating Officer, Margie Kinder, wrote to Sinclair and asked to modify a couple of her responses. It was Sinclair's option to agree or decline the request. Being a conservative, wanting to be accommodating to a fellow conservative, Sinclair allowed Kinder to modify some of the answers to reflect more favorably on her organization. No such request was made of the Patriot-Ombudsman, and the remarks as seen here are the original answers given to the questions.

Then, on the night of Nov. 13, 2013, Akbar began tweeting that Kinder had contacted Sinclair, "demanding a retraction." He followed that with a series of insulting comments about Sinclair and his notorious past, wondering for his Twitter feed readers "why he even bothers to deal with these people who are so beneath him."

The problem is, according to Sinclair, the only request Kinder made was to ask for the modifications that Sinclair made to the responses. Although Sinclair did not identify Kinder in his story (even after being asked by the author to do so), the fact that Akbar identified her made it possible for the author to send an e-mail to Kinder asking if what Akbar said was true – did Kinder "demand a retraction" from Akbar.

Kinder did not respond to my e-mail or to Sinclair's.

This was a real chance to nail Akbar for lying, something Kinder accuses Akbar of doing in her original responses. One of the two men is lying… either Sinclair or Akbar. Kinder had and threw away an opportunity to prove to anyone of the diminishing number of folks who continue to believe everything Akbar says that he is an inveterate liar. Therefore, as the author explained in an email to Kinder, every nickel that Akbar steals from Nov. 14 onward, Kinder will bear part of the responsibility for that theft.

Akbar's Twitter stream since the election has been increasingly bizarre and unhinged. His reactions seem more like a wounded animal, lashing out at anyone who seems like a threat.

The threats are real, and Akbar may – in fact – face some actual danger. Keep in mind, these are only rumors and nothing has been proven, but there is a lot of gossip among the inside-the-Beltway wags that Andrew Breitbart's sudden death on March 1 was not from a random heart attack. There are some who say that Breitbart may have been seen as a rival for Akbar's affections from a super wealthy, super powerful man with scruples that can only be measured by microscope.

Akbar refuses to "dignify" the rumor with comment. (In fact, he refuses to "dignify" any of the numerous charges against him with comment. But his Akbar's case is not helped when people like Karl Rove tell companies like Zazzle to remove images of Akbar because he -- Karl Rove -- owns the intellectual property rights to **Akbar's image!**

But, for now, Akbar is a star. He rose very quickly. And, you are thankful. His ego, like his hubris, has grown to enormous proportions.

But like a comet, there's a chance you will burn out just as quickly. Especially when the Mainstream media starts reporting on the things these intrepid liberal bloggers have been stockpiling.

As the author wrote in his blog at the time:

And I think I got my answer yesterday when KARL ROVE demanded to Zazzle that I remove an image of ALI AKBAR wearing a Barack Obama mask waving fistfuls of $20 bills. We have all heard the rumors about Karl, all the way back to his Nixon years. We all know about the discreet gay clubs in Austin and Washington. And Akbar's orientation is no longer secret. We published a *screen cap photo of him on the gay hookup site "Grindr."*

Now, where I come from (Iowa), 2+2 STILL =4. And the fact that KARL ROVE feels HE has the standing to demand that Zazzle remove an image that does not mention his full name, that contains no PICTURE of Karl Rove, and he claims INTELLECTUAL PROPERTY tells me one of several things.

1. To claim intellectual property, he must have taken the photo.

2. The photo seems to have been taken in a hotel room that nobody else can be seen in.

3. Karl and Ali were alone together in a hotel room.

*4. **Karl's OWN PEOPLE** have been buzzing about Ali and how quickly he rose the totem pole.*

Time to put the cards on the table?

When the going gets rough and people are starting to notice that you might not be all you've advertised yourself to be, what's a boy to do?

How about create a threat against yourself. It was working for Aaron Walker, who blogs under the name Aaron Worthing and raised God knows how much through his blog by telling people he was fired from his job because of terrorist threats from "The Speedway Bomber," Brett Kimberlin, when the fact of the matter is, according to a letter from the lawyer who fired him, Walker was canned for attracting undue attention to his company by being the creator of an "Everybody Draw Mohammed Day" blog – coupled with the fact that Walker was a crappy lawyer who let his actual work go undone while he waged a personal "lawfare" war against Kimberlin,

Pastebin, according to Wikipedia, is a popular online application for coders and folks who frequent the IRC channels where pasting large amounts of text is considered rude.

As of late, it has also been used by folks who have something to say on Twitter, but can't say it within 140 characters.

Such was the case on June 7 when someone identifying himself as Ali Akbar posted what he called **a "threat"** made against him.

Here is the **text of the alleged threat**. There is no clue as to who might have sent it. It is presented here, unedited for spelling or grammar, but with profanity edited to make it suitable for all readers.

"Yo, Ali, you are a liar– you did a years long crime wave, and there is more going to come out. You f**ked me over three years ago, and you are getting your dues now. Dude, you need to resign and go off and hide. Man, the Feds gonna expand their investigation into your crime wave. And you know what I am talking about. I do feel sorry for Mama Lydia, but for you to invoke her on your FB page is disgusting. She is not proud to have a felon turned Uncle Tom and she has told you that many times. If you don't resign, this is going to keep dribbling out and will cross into what you did in other states, and involve drugs — yeah, come on Ali, it was not just some booze. And it could bring down others close to you and you know what I am talkin about. Remember those pictures, or were you too stoned to remember. Well, I remember and I've got the pics. Ali, we used to be tight. You need to walk away dude, now or it's all going to come out. Peeps already talking about you, and they looking to drop some dimes. Walk away now — think of yourself and your family. You already f**ked up enough

things. Dude, you ain't gonna win this one – all the sh*t that you, Mama Lydia and your bro been trying so hard to hide under the rug is gonna come out. You ain't gonna be able to stand no federal investigation."

Akbar Reacts

Akbar was quick to go public -- **very** public -- with this alleged blackmail threat.

The threat was instantly reprinted on a wide variety of right wing blogs. LA Assistant District Attorney Patrick Frey runs the **"Patterico's Pontifications"** blog.

He prints the threat in its entirety. He closes with...

*Again, I will say: **there are mainstream media journalists who are scared to write about this story.** I do not say this lightly. I have been told this is the case.*(Emphasis in original.)

Follow the link to Michelle's column to see what you can do.

Michelle is Michelle Malkin, who many of these bloggers call "The Boss."

What does *she* suggest you do? Among other things...

you can donate to the National Bloggers Club, Inc., which at the time was still referring to itself as a 501(c)3 organization. (Subsequent calls to the IRS proved it was not 501(c)(3) eligible. More on that later).

This alleged blackmail threat found its way all across the conservative Internet. But not once in any of these tales of blackmail does Akbar ever prove that he received an actual threat. He doesn't post the actual e-mail in a screen cap. He doesn't provide the e-mail metadata -- an easy way to see where the e-mail came from. We are left to rely on his word and his word alone that he was threatened.

Telling readers you have been "threatened" and then asking them to send you money to help "protect" you seems to be a central theme among this leftover group of bloggers from the once mighty Andrew Breitbart web empire. Breitbart died March 1 after a sudden heart attack, which right away led to rampant speculation among the so-called "Breitbots" that he had been **murdered on the orders of President Obama**.

Aaron Walker is, perhaps, the best known of the lot. As mentioned earlier, Walker claimed, among other things, that the convicted Speedway Bomber turned left wing activist, Brett Kimberlin, had threatened his life, cost him and his wife their jobs, attempted to murder him, filed "abusive peace orders" to silence him, and had him arrested for violating a standing peace order. At a court hearing July 5, a Montgomery County (Maryland) Court judge lifted a the peace order against Walker, so he is again free to obsess in writing, standing on a street corner or shouting from a roof to complain about Brett Kimberlin's crimes of 30-odd years ago.

Walker was not alone in being threatened by Kimberlin, according to these Breitbart remnants. Walker **wrote**:

*It's not just me. Brett Kimberlin and his anonymous harassing sympathizers have attacked others too, including **Patrick Frey**, Mandy Nagy, Robert McCain, Ali A. Akbar, Brandon Darby and many others.*

If you are worried about Mr. Waker, Mr. Frey, Ms. Nagy, Mr. McCain, Mr. Akbar and Mr. Darby, you can relax. None of them has presented a whiff of proof that they were ever actually threatened. And they will continue to raise money off of the right wing fear that Kimberlin will threaten *them* as well.

In fact, there never was any *proof* offered that Kimberlin

threatened *anyone* since his prison release for the Speedway Bombings in the 1970s. The thing that bothered these right wing bloggers, it would seem, is that Kimberlin objected to the numbers of people, urged on by the right wing bloggers starting way back when Andrew Breitbart was still alive, driving past his house, taking pictures of him and his children, making threatening phone calls, etc. He contended he just wanted to be left alone.

The right wing bloggers did not *want* to leave Mr. Kimberlin alone. They demanded, and have won, what they see as their First Amendment right to tell whatever lie they feel moved to lie about, and to do it while raising money so they can tell more lies without having to get real jobs.

This whole Dead Breitbart, Ali Akbar, Patterico, R. Stacy McCain and Aaron Walker enterprise has been a money-maker for the people involved. In a statement to fans of the National Bloggers Club, Aaron Walker claims to have received $5,000 from people donating to the fund. How much of that money was donated by people who believed their donations were tax deductible? No way to say.

They plan to continue to raise funds from their readership... just in case Kimberlin decides to try again.

As Walker wrote recently:

*When Brett Kimberlin **threatened to sue Patrick Frey** for defaming him by accurately describing his deplorable criminal record, he declared that "I have filed over a hundred lawsuits and another one will be no sweat for me. On the other hand, it will cost you a lot of time and money[.]" His goal is to either successfully silence you, or leave you impoverished as indicated yesterday by an ally of Kimberlin's, **bragging** to me that "[b]y the time this is all said and done, you'll probably be homeless on the streets."*

He won't stop coming after us — after free speech.

Which brings us back to Ali Akbar. He was president and founder of this National Bloggers Club, the group that called itself a 501(c)(3) until enterprising progressive bloggers proved otherwise. Like Walker, Frey, Nagy, McCain, and Darby, he claims to have been viciously and horribly threatened.

No proof, mind you. But isn't his word good enough?

Well, much time has gone by since Akbar posted the threat. Akbar has not resigned from his post. The National Bloggers Club no longer calls itself a 501(c)(3) but it is still raising money hand over fist -- and if you donated to them believing your deduction was tax deductible -- tough luck, kiddo!

5 CALL IN THE BOY-BOINKING LAWYER!

After the alleged threat, Michelle Malkin decided it was time to call in the big guns. Conservative writer Joe Newby remarked about this development in his Jun 7, 2012 story in the online Examiner.com.

On Thursday, Jay Sekulow, Chief Counsel of the **American Center for Law and Justice**(ACLJ), announced that his group would provide legal representation to Ali Akbar and his group, the National Bloggers Club. According to a statement by Sekulow, conservatives affiliated with the organization "are facing threats and intimidation tactics by those opposed to their viewpoint."

"Free speech is under attack," he wrote.

Newby's column continues:

Ali Akbar, president of the National Bloggers Club (NBC), admitted in a **Facebook** note Wednesday that he was charged with felony theft several years ago but did not go to jail.

"Now," he wrote, "sympathizers of convicted domestic terrorist Brett Kimberlin are harassing me, tearing me apart—and coming after my family.

"In the past two weeks, hackers have tried accessing my email accounts, they've placed a fake SWAT call on a colleague, and just two days ago they posted the address and picture of my mother's home in an attempt to incite unlawful behavior—or violence," he added.

According to Akbar, the harassment is due to fundraising efforts by his group designed "to relieve some of Aaron Walker's financial strife—caused by his own legal run-in with Kimberlin." Akbar said.

"Despite all of this," Akbar **wrote**, "I'll stand for free speech. We're going to get the peace order against Walker overturned, restore his First Amendment rights, and fight the thugs who are bullying my family."

The "bullying" of Akbar's family consisted of an

anonymous blog post, plus a photograph of the house Akbar's mother, Lydia Dews, owns in Fort Worth, Texas. It is the address Akbar gives as the site of incorporation for the documents filed to create the National Bloggers Club.

A simple rule – if you don't want your address made public, don't include it on a publicly-available document.

And what did Malkin and Akbar get for their involvement with the ACLJ?

More scandal!

By late September, one of the ACLJ's senior counsels found himself embroiled in a web of sex, prostitution, drugs and other naughty stuff that we might not have noticed had it not been for the group's defense of the National Blogger's Club.

Enter James. M. Henderson, Sr.

Conservative Stalwart, Stood with Terri Schaivo's Parents

Senior Counsel for the American Center for Law and Justice

Defender of Conservative Blogger Ali Akbar, National Bloggers Club

Adjunct Professor at Pat Robertson's Regent University Law School

Youth Minister at His Church

When the American Center for Law and Justice signed a "Friend of the Court" brief in an attempt to extend the

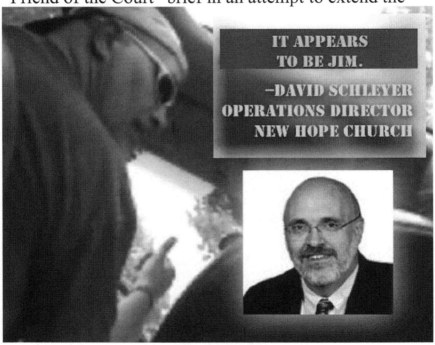

life of Terri Schaivo in their lawsuit against the state of Florida, one of the signatures at the bottom was that of noted Constitutional Attorney James M. Henderson, Sr. His name was also on a "Friend of the Court" brief filed in the case of Bush v. Gore in which he sided with the team urging the US Supreme Court to reverse the Florida Supreme Court's decision to restart the recount. A Senior Counsel with the American Center for Law and Justice (ACLJ) and Adjunct Professor of Law at Regent University School of Law — the university founded by Pat Robertson — Conservative stalwart James M. Henderson, Sr., seems like an unlikely person to be tied into a gay sex scandal involving several young men.

Yet that would seem to be the information uncovered by an investigation published Monday night, Sept. 24, by an online group of anonymous writers publishing under the name "Exposed Politics".

The website doesn't rely on hearsay or innuendo. They have pictures. They had video. They had chat transcripts.

The arch-Conservative, staunchly-Christian ACLJ states its mission "is dependent upon God and the resources He provides through the time, talent, and gifts of people who share our concerns and desire to protect our religious and constitutional freedoms." Yes, this is the same ACLJ that trumpeted in June that they would "defend free speech in the blogosphere" by "representing top conservative bloggers targeted for harassment."

Remember?

The ACLJ is representing Ali Akbar, a top blogger and president of the National Bloggers Club, a coalition of 300 conservative bloggers who reach millions of readers. Akbar has seen his mother's home photographed and placed on the internet. He has also received formal notification that he may soon be sued for publishing truthful information about radical liberals and their wealthy donors.

The irony of this is, Henderson was ultimately ratted out to Exposed Politics, it would seem, by one of his young pals.

The young man who ratted him out uses the a cell phone video to get Henderson to explain how he came up with the name Kyle Johnson.

Roger Shuler, owner of the Legal Schnauzer law blog said:

Sounds like a classic case of conservative hypocrisy. And Mr. Henderson is hardly a back-bencher. He has been involved in some of the biggest issues of our day. You can do a little Web research and find him assisting with legal briefs on cases involving First Amendment, abortion, Obamacare, and much more. It looks like he has been involved with Focus on the Family. This is a guy who has gone to a lot of effort to shape our society according to his right-wing vision. Now, it appears his vision includes smoking weed and chasing young boys.

When his law firm found out, the ACLJ acted quickly. His biography, his information on the writers' page, the cases he worked on, his very life as a member, an IMPORTANT member of the American Center for Law and Justice?

Erased. He was rendered a non-person. Despite our best efforts we could never get a response from Henderson or any of his former cohorts at the ACLJ. It wasn't until Metro Weekly, D.C.'s gay magazine, wrote the story we sent them to investigate that the ACLJ even admitted that Henderson was dismissed.

If Henderson intends to claim that he was fired for being gay, he will first have to prove that he is, in fact, a legitimate gay person or bisexual. It is possible for people who are completely heterosexual in orientation to give in to the temptation to have sex with younger people of the same sex. It's a condition called ephebophilia, which is defined as the primary or exclusive adult sexual interest in mid-to-late adolescents, generally ages 15 to 19. The term has been described by French writer Félix Buffière in 1980 and Pakistani scholar Tariq Rahman, who argued that "ephebophilia" should be used in preference to "homosexuality" when describing the aesthetic and erotic interest of adult men in adolescent boys in classical Persian, Turkish or Urdu literature.

According to a scholarly publication, "Heterosexual Interest in Homosexual Males," an ephebophiliac man is not necessarily homosexual.

The subject of older, heterosexual men being attracted to the effeminate qualities of younger, homosexual males is deeply entrenched in ancient and contemporary culture.

But regardless, ACLJ would likely find itself in the position of having to defend itself against the charge that they fired Henderson strictly because he was gay, not because of the negative publicity that came with the revelation that he was cruising for young men. If his behavior was strictly with young men age 18 and over, it would be considered "adultery" which is considered by evangelicals to be a sin, and someone bringing negative publicity to a law firm by committing adultery, especially at a law firm known to be a right wing, Christian conservative evangelical law firm, it seems to the casual observer that Henderson will have a tough time proving his case..

From the videotape in which Zach Payne (who was 19 at the time) captured Henderson's identity:

ZACH: Why such a random name?
KYLE: Which one?
ZACH: Kyle Johnson, why such a random name?

If the predator has to ask his prey which name he is known by, one can imagine he has a whole rolodex of young men who knew him under different identities.

How this will affect the ACLJ's defense of the National Blogger's Club remains to be seen. But it sure shows that Michelle Malkin knows how to pick 'em.

But Newby was correct in his reporting. In a June 6, 2012 letter to his fan base, published on **his Facebook page**, shortly after his past criminal activity was revealed to his adoring public, rising Tea Party star Akbar lied about the circumstances of his arrest and incarceration in 2007 and scolded his critics for placing his mother in danger.

In the past two weeks, hackers have tried accessing my email accounts, they've placed a fake SWAT call on a colleague, and just two days ago they posted the address and picture of my mother's home in an attempt to incite unlawful behavior—or violence.

An attempt to incite unlawful behavior -- or violence? Not so much. **It was to show the legally listed headquarters of Akbar's "Vice and Victory" agency.**

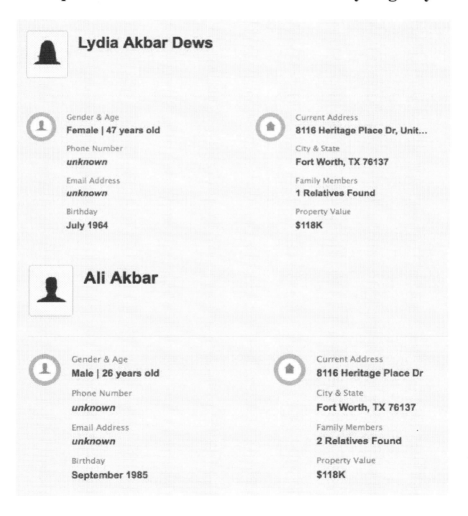

Lydia Akbar Dews

Gender & Age	Current Address
Female | 47 years old	**8116 Heritage Place Dr, Unit...**
Phone Number	City & State
unknown	**Fort Worth, TX 76137**
Email Address	Family Members
unknown	**1 Relatives Found**
Birthday	Property Value
July 1964	**$118K**

Ali Akbar

Gender & Age	Current Address
Male | 26 years old	**8116 Heritage Place Dr**
Phone Number	City & State
unknown	**Fort Worth, TX 76137**
Email Address	Family Members
unknown	**2 Relatives Found**
Birthday	Property Value
September 1985	**$118K**

Yes. The address for the Vice and Victory Agency happens to be the same address as Akbar's mother.

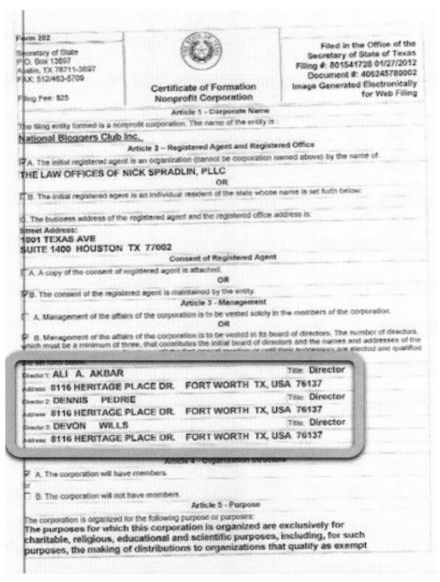

It also happens to be the same address for the National Bloggers Club, the organization created by Akbar which he, at first, listed as a tax-exempt 501(c)(3) status until this writer and others contacted the IRS and learned that the organization did not have the legal right to claim such status. In fact, the Texas Certificate of Formation of a Not Profit Corporation shows 8116 Heritage Place Drive, Fort Worth, Texas, not only as Akbar's address, but as the address of two of the other players in this little Telenovela -- John Dennis Pedrie and Devon Wills.

(Another interesting sidebar – we attempted to contact Nick Spradlin, the lawyer who is listed on the incorporation papers. He told us he does not represent Akbar any more, and he told us to never, ever, never call his office again. Hmm.)

This is a bunch we first met when the blogger Breitbart Unmasked introduced them in a June 4, 2012 post.

A number of right wing bloggers who claim they are the National Bloggers Club have recently been attacking Brett Kimberlin in mass accusing him of every dirty deed in the book. So, because of that, we here at BU decided to check into this National Bloggers Club to see who was behind

it, and what their mission is, and also who funded who, or where the money came from to run this loose knit operation of right wing bloggers who use the internet to raise money for causes they create, and or basically wreck havoc with anyone considered an enemy of their little group.

First up is Ali A. Akbar.

Ali and his childhood friends are directors of the National Bloggers Club. However they don't all live at this address above. I find it strange they all do not live or even work at this address, yet file corporate forms with the State and IRS that claim that they all live or reside or work at this address. The issue here is that most of these people running this company are just young kids in their early 20's who have scant to zero business experience and seem to not know the landscape of the business world or how to operate in it. But that is just my opinion.

Then there is the affable John Dennis Pedrie as one of the Directors of The National Bloggers Club. His claim to fame was that he worked until 2010 at the Onyx Ice Arena as an Ice Rink Maintenance Man. So he went from Ice

Maintenance worker to Vice President of Technology and Development at Vice & Victory, which is another Ali Akbar creation, to one of the Directors of The National Bloggers Club. Wow, sounds like he has some real corporate experience behind him.

Programmer
Aria Ventures, LLC
Venture Capital & Private Equity industry
Currently holds this position

Vice President, Technology and Development
Vice and Victory Agency, LLC
Public Company; 1-10 employees; Public Relations and Communications industry
January 2011 – October 2011 (10 months)

Programmer
Profitable Results Marketing
October 2009 – March 2011 (1 year 6 months)

VP of Vendor Services
Republic Modern Media
September 2008 – January 2011 (2 years 5 months)
We make websites and run eCampaigns.

Ice Maintenance
The Onyx Rochester Ice Arena
October 2007 – January 2010 (2 years 4 months)
I drive a Zamboni

Then we go to Devon Wills, who's claim to fame was that he was a personal shopper at J Crew before he became the CEO at Wills Group LLC, and then later a Director of The National Bloggers Club.

Right now he is going to the all Christian stud Liberty University which was founded by the Reverend Jerry Falwell, and which claims in its mission statement that it trains Champions for Christ.

There are a number of others who are in the process of signing up for a National Bloggers Club board seat; such as Michelle Malkin who has also been a front runner in leading the

Experience

CEO
The Wills Group LLC
November 2011 – Present (8 months) | Lynchburg, Virginia Area

Account Manager
Republic Modern Media LLC
March 2010 – January 2011 (11 months)

Republic Modern Media is a new media-consulting firm for right-of-center political organizations, special interest groups, and political campaigns. I acted as liaison between the clients and the company.

Personal Shopper
J.Crew
Privately Held, 5001-10,000 employees; JCG; Retail industry
March 2009 – March 2010 (1 year 1 month)

Was sole point of contact for clients, to give them a more personal experience with the company. Gave styling advice and direction on merchandise.

Devon Wills
CEO at The Wills Group, LLC
Lynchburg, Virginia | Public Relations and Communications

Current	CEO at The Wills Group LLC
Past	Account Manager at Republic Modern Media LLC
	Personal Shopper at J.Crew
Education	Liberty University
	Southwest Baptist University
Connections	99 connections
Websites	Company Website
Public Profile	http://www.linkedin.com/in/devonwills

Share	PDF	Print	Flag

charge against Brett Kimberlin in the media. Of course we will post more data on this organization as the crow flies here at BU. The one interesting connection was who was the money man that seeded the National Bloggers

Club? Well, that just so happens to be Foster Friess. Foster is another right wing corporate billionaire who has given money to the Koch Brothers, and also claims he also helps out American Crossroads which is run by Karl Rove.

(FROM THE WIKIPEDIA ENTRY ON FOSTER FRIESS)

Friess has been an active patron of religious and conservative causes. He has been instrumental in keeping the political campaign of the 2012 presidential hopeful Rick Santorum alive by financing a super PAC, the Red, White and Blue Fund, which runs television advertisements on behalf of Santorum, who was unable to run a television campaign with his own funds. According to campaign filings with the Federal Election Commission, Friess's contributions to the Red, White and Blue Fund amount to more than 40% of its total assets – or, $331,000 as of 31 December 2011.[5][6]He had donated $250,000 to Santorum's re-election campaign in 2006, and at least that amount to the Republican Governors' Association.[7] In the wake of the New Hampshire Republican primary, 2012, and before the South Carolina primary, Friess told Politico that he was "putting together a challenge grant to encourage other wealthy donors to give to the Red, White and Blue Fund, … he said [the fund] received a $1 million check" the day after the New Hampshire vote.[8] The Million-dollar donation was conveyed in four checks between November, 2011 and January, 2012.[6]

In addition to Santorum's faith, pro-life stance, and hawkish foreign policy leanings, the possibility of defeating incumbent President Barack Obama was a major component of Friess's decision to back Santorum's campaign.[9] Friess is reportedly considering major contributions to American Crossroads in hopes to influence key 2012 senate races.[10]

Friess has also donated $100,000 to Wisconsin Governor Scott Walker to help defeat the Democrats' recall effort in 2011. In addition, he has reportedly donated more than $3 million to the conservative commentator Tucker Carlson's The Daily Caller website.[7] At one of the semi-annual, private seminars held by the Koch brothers in June 2011, Friess was recognized for his donation exceeding $1 million to the Kochs' political activities.[11]

The other interesting connection was this Yahoo News article on the private invite only meeting that started the National Bloggers Club.

James O'Keefe attending the opening bash of the National Bloggers Club and claiming Fuck the media? Well James I think you have that

wrong, it's not fuck the media, it's the media fucks you. But that is just how I look at it.

Organizers used the party to announce the formation of a new nonprofit started with seed money from millionaire Santorum-backer Foster Friess. Called the "National Bloggers Club," the group will use donations to fund private reporting projects. It also hopes to issue press passes, serving as a clearinghouse so event organizers can differentiate between a blogger with honest intentions versus someone looking for a free pass by starting a Blogspot account. But mostly, the organizers said, the new organization will support and encourage online writers.

"On the left, they take care of their own. They respect their own," Clouthier said. "They take care of their bloggers."

At the party at Microsoft on Thursday night, the bartenders served up free cocktails and beer while the rock band Madison Rising played a live set. Near the end of the night, Blog Bash organizers announced an awards ceremony, during which filmmaker James O'Keefe was granted a "Sunlight" prize for a short film revealing how easy he believes it is to vote in New Hampshire under a false name.

A hero on the right and a villain to the left, O'Keefe walked to the front of the room, grabbed the microphone and pretty much summed up the night.

"I say," O'Keefe said, after thanking the group for the award, "Fuck the media!"

So what do we have here? We have Foster Friess starting the National Bloggers Club with James O'Keefe attending, with connections to the Koch Brothers and Karl Rove. We also have media personalities such as Michele Malkin who is also connected to Robert Stacy McCain. We also have Ali Akbar who is connected to the rest of the right wing bloggers, and who have all been attacking in mass one guy by the name of Brett Kimberlin, who I might add has been on a

many years long crusade to expose the corruption behind Karl Rove and the Koch Brothers and James O'Keefe. I would call these connections very interesting indeed. What I also find even more interesting is that they have recently been raising money for a few bloggers who they claim are under the threat of some future lawsuit, yet, they have a billionaire funding them. So my question is why do they need to raise funds for some future legal challenges when they have such heavy guns seeding them with huge resources of money? Why not just call up Foster Friess and ask him for the money to support Robert Stacy McCain and Mandy Nagy and the millionaire John Patrick Frey? Those are very interesting questions which we will probe into in the days ahead.

Oddly enough, that address given on the document is also listed as the location of something called Celixion Lightweight Division. A thorough check of Google Directories gives no clue as to what kind of business it is.

The various directories list it as an "unclassified business". A Spokeo reverse phone number search takes one to the home of an 80-year old man living in Midlothian, Texas. A Google search of the man's name along with the word Celixion comes back with 0 results. Yet, all the listings online for Celixion Lightweight Division list that phone number.

The address was also, at one time, listed as the registrant address for Ray McKinney.org, but that was before Akbar dropped him like a hot rock after he lost in the 2010 General Election in Georgia.

Could that be where Mr. Akbar met Mr. Rove?

It is also the address Vice and Victory used to make their $750 "sponsorship donation" to the **"Republican State Leadership Committee."**

It is also the address Akbar gives to **register a website called** "AliAkbar.net" which now directs to his **Twitter page**.

But please, don't mock the young poet. He wrote this seven years ago.

The Desert

i've been wondering, oh i've been wondering.this path
has been long and hard and it keeps going.not a soul out
there, but me.

people tell me how to live and how to get off this path.but
what do they know, they've never been here before.but i
still got that one friend.

how long 'til Heaven, oh God?how long must i
suffer?how long will i question.

there's salvation, there's redemption, there's communion.i
just can't see it from here.

in the desert.no man in sight, no God in sight.but he's
watching over me, this i know.

ali a. akbar

Ah, the angst of youth.

Which brings us back to Akbar's original letter to his
Facebook followers. Let's take the statement and counter
it with the facts as proven here and elsewhere.

One night, a friend asked to be taken to work, but first he wanted to stop by the ATM. I was "the guy with the car," so after dropping off my other friends, I rushed him to the ATM. He was already late to work, and had become irritated. He had a bad temper so my goal was to simply keep the situation calm and under control. He kept sliding the card through, typed in his pin, but for whatever reason he couldn't get funds out. On the drive to drop him off he explained to me that it was not his card. It belonged to his previous roommate and he said the person owed him money. Shame and horror fell over me—and it still does.

So, why does the indictment from the grand jury claim you broke into a guy's truck, stole his debit card and tried to use it? It says nothing about Akbar "giving a guy a ride" and "he used the card." The indictment says Akbar broke into a truck and Akbar used the card.

Although no funds were withdrawn, a crime was committed and it was the second run in with this very same friend. And I stayed silent. A few months later, after I had gotten back on my feet and reconciled with my family, I learned a valuable lesson when detectives came to my door: actions have consequences—no matter how far down the road. Pridefully, I refused my mother's advice and was uncooperative with the police. **I refused to turn in my friend, so I became an associate.** *I broke my mother's heart and undermined the work she had done in the legal community over the years—not to mention a lifetime of raising her son to be a better man.*

I think the word he was looking for is "accomplice." But he is not charged with being an accomplice. He is charged with committing the crime. He was the only person charged.

Thank God, the judicial system was kind—and although there's a horrible mugshot of me, **(at least three, in fact -- Author.)** *I was treated well—better than I thought I deserved. We separated two instances over the course of a year. The Judge, assistant District Attorney, and my lawyers gathered in a room and worked out an arrangement. They shielded me from the shame of being herded around in the system or* **sent to jail***. My work in the community and my academic record bought me a little goodwill. Despite all this, I was still charged with felony theft.*

So, why does the arrest record say that Akbar was incarcerated in the Tarrant County jail? Are *they* liars? Or is Akbar?

Akbar's every dealing with the public has shown a pattern of deception, self-aggrandizement, and a propensity towards separating fools from their money.

It's one thing to make a legitimate claim that people are harassing your mother. It's quite another thing, and shows a certain layer of hypocrisy, cynicism, and downright dishonesty, to whine to your followers that people are picking on your mommy when you are doing business as a right wing organization, raising thousands of dollars by illegally claiming tax-exempt status, and trying to affect election outcomes from your mommy's house.

6 INTELLECTUAL PROPERTY?

This is the photo that Karl Rove demanded that Zazzle remove from its product lineup. Karl Rove & Co. claimed "intellectual property rights" on the image. Rove is not seen in the image.

Neither Ali Akbar nor Karl Rove has commented on the photo, despite several attempts to reach them for comment.

A closer look at the photo raises more questions than it answers.

For one thing, the photo as shown on Ali Akbar's Facebook page was originally a mirror image. There are two ways we are aware of to get a mirror image of a photo.

1. Take the photo into a mirror. But if that were the case here, the flash would have obliterated the image.

2. Take a photo. Use photo software to flip the image and make it appear as if it were taken in a mirror. Hope the people viewing the photo are not aware of the aforementioned "flash" issue.

It's impossible to tell where the photo was taken. At first, we believed it was a hotel room. But after closer inspection, we see what looks like a home entertainment wireless satellite speaker in the lower left corner. And our own experience with hotel rooms has led us to very few places where overhead lighting is controlled with a pull cord.

The flash in the image raises many salacious questions. It is clear the flash originated from below and close to Mr. Akbar. About belt level is our best guess. See how the underside of Mr. Akbar's fingers are illuminated while the upper sides are in shadow. See the angle of the flash reflection on the plastic mask.

Thank you for allowing us to be of service to you.

Subject

Public Product Inquiry: 176147633196511686

Discussion Thread

Response Via Email(Mike) - 07/02/2012 03:43 PM
Hello Zazzler,

Thank you for being a Seller at Zazzle.com!

We would love to offer every design that our users submit, however we must abide by all applicable laws and standards as well as our own content guidelines and copyright policies.

Unfortunately, it appears that your products titled, "pretend time is fun", does not meet Zazzle's Acceptable Content Guidelines. Specifically, your product infringes upon the intellectual property rights of Karl Rove.

Zazzle has been contacted by by representatives by Karl Rove & Co., www.rove.com, and at their request, to remove designs that may infringe upon their rights from the Zazzle Marketplace.

We are sorry for any disappointment, but hope you will understand our position in this regard. For future reference, please review Zazzle's Acceptable Content Guidelines at: http://zazzle.custhelp.com/app/answers/detail/a_id/143.

If you have any further questions, please don't hesitate to contact us.

Thanks for using Zazzle. We look forward to seeing more of your creative designs!

Best Regards,
Mike
Content Management Team
Zazzle, Inc.

Customer By Email (Zazzler Groucheteria) - 07/02/2012 03:41 PM
Again, I have to ask, who owns the picture? Whose intellectual property did I violate if I created the graphic?

Again, we return to the image and to Mr. Rove's claim of "intellectual property rights." We have examined how a person can claim intellectual property rights to an image. Best we can determine, generally speaking, according to

American copyright law, intellectual property rights go to the person taking the photo. Therefore, Karl Rove would have to have taken the photo to claim such a right. And one could rightfully ask, why was Karl Rove so close and at belt level to Ali Akbar while he was wearing an Obama mask waving $20 bills at him.

But if Rove owns the rights to the image, hasn't Akbar violated those rights? After all, the picture was not taken from a Karl Rove website. **It was taken from Ali Akbar's Facebook page.**

According to Facebook's "Statement of Rights and Responsibilities"

Paragraph 2: Sharing Your Information

Subparagraph 4: When you publish content or information using the Public setting, it means that **you are allowing everyone, including people off of Facebook, to access and use that information, and to associate it with you** (i.e., your name and profile picture).

(Emphasis added)

Again, the fact that Ali Akbar posted the image on his

Facebook Page in a Public setting negates Karl Rove's intellectual property rights claim, does it not? Nowhere on the photo in its original Facebook setting does Akbar claim "photo used with permission of Karl Rove & Co."

Again, these are simple questions that could be easily answered by either Ali Akbar or Karl Rove, should they choose to answer the questions we have directed to them through their websites and e-mail addresses. As of this writing, they have not responded.

So, folks are free to come to their own conclusions.

Ali Abdul Razaq Akbar, the rising star of the young Republican firmament, maintains his refusal to answer any direct questions about his alleged connection with Karl Rove, why Karl Rove claimed "intellectual property rights" over an image on Akbar's Facebook page, or any improprieties surrounding the formation of his latest effort to separate his followers from their money -- the National Bloggers Club, Inc., which he at first claimed was a 501(c)(3) tax exempt organization, a claim that was refuted by the IRS.

Now comes word that the IRS has officially begun its investigation into the activities of the National Bloggers

Club., Inc. A letter signed by Nanette M. Downing, IRS director of Exempt Organization Examinations, says:

Thank you for the information you submitted regarding National Bloggers Club, Inc. The Internal Revenue Service has an ongoing examination program to ensure that exempt organizations comply with the applicable provisions of the Internal Revenue Code. The information you submitted will be considered in this program.

In his Twitter stream, Akbar reacted with outrage when a friend of his made casual mention to a previous Examiner story.

At about 10pm ET on July 10, Dina Fraioli tweeted...

Well this can't be good for "@ali" http://is.gd/SyBJC3

The story she linked to is the one about how Mr. Ali may have more explaining to do about his denied connection to a PAC that he clearly was working with during the failed Ray McKinney congressional campaign in the Georgia 12th district in 2010.

This tweet by Dina did not sit at all well with Mr. Akbar.

.@DinaFraioli are you serious? Using a mentally ill

liberal Blogger to attack me Dina? Classless.

"Mentally ill blogger?" This was not a blog Dina linked to. It was a legitimate news story at Examiner.com.

Dina responded:

@ali I'm more amused than serious. Should have added a □#eyeroll

But Akbar wasn't having it.

.@DinaFraioli this crowd has used criminal harassment against me + several others. And that's funny? This dude is a Stalker and u encourage

Nixon probably thought Woodward and Bernstein were stalkers, too. Same with Edward R. Murrow and Sen. Joe McCarthy. Dina continued to try to make light of the situation.

@ali and come on, I'm not classless, I'm a bitch... at least get it right. :)

But Akbar's outrage would not be so easily charmed away.

Really disgusted by anyone trying to empower

☐#BrettKimberlin ☐'s trolls. Very real dangers.

This is part of Akbar's contention that anyone who would dare mention his name in anything less than a glowing and fawning fashion must, in fact, be in the employ of Brett Kimberlin. More about that in a moment, but first -- Dina tried again.

@ali No, dear. I'm amused that he's gone through those lengths to attack you.

"Lengths?" Hardly. Publicly available information. Dina could have written the same series of stories. But then she takes issue with a comment Akbar made about this reporter.

@ali Also, "Mentally ill" when did that become something you use to attack someone? SO Tacky.

Akbar attempted to justify his characterization of this writer.

@DinaFraioli he literally is. It's not an accusation, it's his condition. And I'm not amused. Live my life for a quick minute.

Now, let's be clear. This writer does not have a mental

illness. This writer has, and has been quite public about, been diagnosed with Parkinson's disease since 2000. It is a movement disorder, not a mental illness. More facts on the disease are available at The **National Parkinson Foundation**, the organization this writer was trying to raise money for when Karl Rove claimed intellectual property rights on an image of Akbar and forced its removal from the online gift store on **Zazzle**.

Now, "paranoia"? That *is* classified as a mental condition.

These attacks from Ali Akbar are typical of the group that once orbited around the gravitational forces of the late Andrew Breitbart, the well-read conservative blogger who died suddenly on March 1. Any criticism is immediately taken as an attack by the nefarious forces of convicted Speedway Bomber turned liberal activist Brett Kimberlin. The "criminal attacks" Ali speaks of include the asking of questions he does not want to answer, the publication of a picture of his mother's house *(explained by the fact that Akbar listed the address as his place of business in his filing for the National Bloggers Club, as well as the address for all of his various websites created under the "Vice & Victory" agency he created),* and -- perhaps -- certain cloud formations that he somehow determines were formed by Kimberlin and everyone who ever spoke his name in an effort to somehow harm Akbar.

Mr. Akbar could clear all this up in an hour or so if he would agree to be questioned. But he steadfastly refuses to answer hard questions from actual journalists and instead pretends that everyone who wants to know the real story of how an ex-con sitting in a jail cell in 2007 could rise so quickly to the rank of Young Republican Icon with no college, no visible means of support, without someone in a position of power "taking care" of him in some fashion.

These are real questions that require real answers, and Mr. Akbar continues to do a disservice to himself and his various right wing causes by continuing to duck and dodge reality.

Some months later, however, Karl Rove floated to the top of the pool and addressed the controversy.

The author received an answer from the online "make your own t-shirt store" Zazzle.com regarding why they removed a design of his and claimed it was the intellectual property of Karl Rove.

It was all a mistake.

Yeah. You see, on July 2 when "Mike" at the Content Review office of the popular online store Zazzle sent the author 36 separate e-mails (one for each product bearing this design) that they were being removed from the shelves because the design was someone's intellectual property, the author responded by asking just whose intellectual property he was stepping on.

The folks at Zazzle were quick to respond.

The author attempted to get a response from Mr. Rove or someone in his office to explain why Rove would claim intellectual property to an image in which he was not pictured, unless he was the photographer thereof.

Two months later, Lori Moore, an investigative journalist from Alabama, looking into the railroading of Gov. Don Siegleman, found out about this little kerfuffle and wrote to Rove & Company. She received an almost immediate reply.

So, the author wrote directly to the Rove flack and received the same answer. After several back and forth e-mails with the Rove flack playing word games, we posted the actual image and asked a direct yes or no question.

Did Karl Rove & Company order Zazzle to remove this particular image?

No way to weasel around that one.

The flack wrote back.

"No, we did not ask Zazzle to remove the image."

Oh ho! So now all the author had to do was contact Zazzle, get a copy of the takedown order and prove Rove's flack was a liar.

Except...

After waiting for hours, Zazzle came back with an excuse that reminds a father of seeing a child standing next to a broken cookie jar, crumbs on his face and shirt, telling daddy that a monster broke the cookie jar and he chased the monster away.

Observe.

To sum up, here is what Zazzle wants us to believe.

1. In late June 2012 the author opened a store on Zazzle that -- at the time -- had but one design image. This image. It is GOP operative and ex-con Ali Akbar, widely rumored at the time to be Karl Rove's "very good friend" (which is as good a euphemism as we care to use this morning), wearing a Barack Obama mask, waving money in the face of whoever is taking the photo, a person whom, given the angle of the flash, is using a camera phone at or near Akbar's belt level.

2. For some reason, Zazzle receives what they called a "takedown order" for this image, and removes all 36 or so items that bore the image from the the author's store.

3. Zazzle informs the author that Karl Rove and Company demanded the design's removal.

4. The author writes to Rove through various channels, gets no reply.

5. The intrepid and doggedly determined Lori Moore, an investigative reporter from Alabama stumbles across the author's story while doing research on how Karl Rove may have been involved in former Alabama Governor Don's Siegleman's railroading into jail. Using the same contact form as the author, she contacts Rove's office and gets a nearly immediate reply saying "we don't remove items that are not our intellectual property."

6. The author contacts the Rove Flack and after several back and forth e-mails where the flack parses and dances around words, she answers a direct yes or no question. "No, we did not order the design's removal."

7. The author contacts Zazzle and asks them to look at their takedown order to see who ordered the item removed.

8. Several hours later, the mealy-mouthed reply from Zazzle that it was all a mistake and they got a takedown order from Rove but it wasn't meant to include the author's design and they took it down by mistake, but

then at the author's request, they contacted Rove's flack who told him *"these are not the droids you are looking for"* and now, all of a sudden, the takedown order that ordered the takedown of the author's item was NOT a takedown order of the author's item and now it's back up online for everyone to buy it, ha ha, hey hey, ho, mistakes happen.

9. The author, knowing when he is being lied to, wrote back to Zazzle demanding to see a copy of the original takedown order to see who demanded the item be removed from his store. No reply.

Were the author a suspicious sort, he might wonder whether or not Rove's sudden "Jedi Mind Trick" on Zazzle is related to the fact that Rove apparently has moved on from his "very good friend" relationship with convicted debit fraudster Ali Akbar and is now plowing new and more profitable farmland -- so to speak. This means, one could suppose, that Mr. Akbar has been abandoned by what some believe has been his "Sugar Daddy" since those heady days when they met in South Carolina and, suddenly, Akbar went from campaign hanger-on to running his own business, bereft of education, a visible source of income, or anything in his favor other than his good looks.

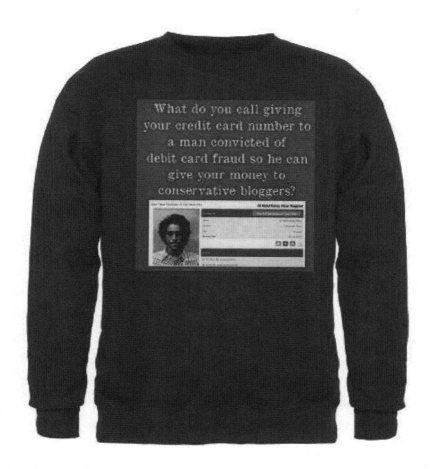

What do you call giving your credit card number to a man convicted of debit card fraud so he can give your money to conservative bloggers?

Karl Rove doesn't seem to have all that much influence with Cafe Press.

The author was not the only person suspicious about Karl Rove and the rumored affair with Akbar. Blogger Roger

Shuler at "The Legal Schnauzer" had questions as well in a June 27 post.

Karl Rove is having a bisexual affair with the president of a conservative bloggers' group, and concern about being outed sparked Rove's falsehood-filled diatribe last week on Greta Van Susteren's Fox News program.

Rove's lover is Ali Akbar, president of the National Bloggers Club, an umbrella group that grew from the activism of the late right-wing publisher and pundit Andrew Breitbart. A left-leaning Web site called Breitbart Unmasked recently disclosed that Akbar has a criminal record that includes convictions for credit-card fraud, theft, and burglary.

The stunning allegations about Rove and Akbar are included in a letter sent yesterday from Alabama attorney Dana Jill Simpson to Robert Bauer, counsel for President Barack Obama's 2012 re-election campaign. The letter also includes an appeal for a presidential pardon on behalf of former Alabama Governor Don Siegelman.

Rove, appearing with Van Susteren on the June 20 edition of On the Record, took a question about the tax-exempt status of certain PACs and turned it into an attack on Simpson, Bauer, and Siegelman--who was the target of perhaps the most notorious political prosecution in U.S. history.

Simpson, a former GOP operative, is best known as a whistleblower in the Siegelman case. She has stated under oath and testified before Congress that she participated in a telephone conference call with prominent Alabama Republicans who discussed plans to bring bogus criminal charges against

Siegelman, apparently with Rove's approval.

Rove told Van Susteren that Bauer represented Simpson in her 2007 testimony before Congress and that Simpson did not testify under oath. It's a matter of public record that Simpson made sworn statements about the Siegelman prosecution on multiple occasions. And Simpson included in her letter to Bauer yesterday an affidavit stating that he has never represented her, and the two have never met. (See the affidavit and letter at the end of this post.) Bauer has sent a letter to Rove demanding a retraction, according to a report in Huffington Post.

Why would Rove become so wildly disengaged from the truth, on a national television program where he was asked a question that had nothing to do with Jill Simpson? The Alabama lawyer says in her letter to Bauer that Rove became unhinged because he knew she had damaging information about his personal life--and it soon might become public knowledge.

At the heart of Rove's discomfort is his relationship with Ali Akbar. And how did that come to light?

Simpson spells it out in her letter to Bauer:

About a week and a half ago, I was contacted by a political operative on the left who gave me a copy of Ali Akbar's advertisement on an adult website. This advertisement suggested that the National Bloggers Club President, Mr. Akbar, was looking for bisexual sex with men who were Republican, political, and loved to discuss politics and philosophy and just wanted to hang out and chill with them.

Simpson has an e-mail list on which she periodically shares inside information on politics and international affairs. The Akbar ad became a subject for discussion on the list. Andrew Kreig, of the D.C.-based Justice-Integrity Project, briefly referenced the Akbar angle in a major piece about Rove's statements on the Van Susteren show. Kreig did not mention Akbar by name, but he did write the following:

In a similar vein, Rove critics active in the blogosphere have been claiming over the past week that one of Rove's colleagues is an ex-con who might be outed soon in a sex scandal. This is part of the ongoing back-and-forth war of nerves that political activists wage continually against one another, with lawsuits and claims of outrage by each side. Among the latter are GOP members of Congress seeking Justice Department prosecutions of liberal opponents.

In this context, it made sense for Rove to deflect attacks by claiming to Fox listeners that he has been cleared from any suspicions by previous investigations and that critics are partisans allied unfairly against him.

In her letter to Bauer, Simpson says she took the
Akbar ad and used it to unearth information about
his ties to powerful Republicans. One of those, the
letter suggests, is Rove:

**I took [the information] back to my
blogging group and showed them that
Karl had gotten himself a new friend from
the information and evidence I had
received and that this guy was alleged to
be the possible new boy wonder and lover
of Karl Rove.**

Simpson tells Bauer that she has no concerns about
Rove's sexual preferences, but she is alarmed
about his multiple false statements on Fox News:

**It is believed by many of us that Karl
thought we were going to use this for the
benefit of President Obama, which was**

never the case. We do not care if [Rove] is bisexual or not and have many times ignored information that was given to us that suggested that he is. In fact, we find nothing wrong with being bisexual, as it means people just love both sexes at the same time. All of us are LBGTQ supporters, so we elected to not out this information on him. However, I think this is why he went berserk on national TV on Fox Network and said that I am a liar and have disappeared. He also lied when he said I had never testified under oath, as I have. It is Mr. Rove who insisted on executive privilege so as to not have to testify under oath about the Siegelman case.

Simpson states that something positive could come from Rove's appearance on the Van Susteren program:

With all that said, I am very grateful that Mr. Rove was hung up about having his alleged bisexuality possibly released that he pointed out on National TV, not once but twice, that you are a man who can possibly get things done in the Obama Administration. For that reason I am asking you to please consider joining us . . . [in] asking President Obama to pardon Don Siegelman. As you may recall, I was the individual that Karl Rove asked to follow Don Siegelman to a party in Alabama to try to catch him cheating with a gay man in his administration named Nick Bailey.

Does all of this have national implications? Simpson says the answer is yes, and she urges Bauer to take action:

In closing, I just want to say that I am sad you got dragged into this, but I am

happy that you now know beyond a shadow of a doubt that Karl Rove lied on you, me, and Mr. Siegelman. It is time that someone in the Obama Administration stopped this monster maniac from hurting innocent people--and I hope that man is you.

Ali A. Akbar @ali   4h
Side note: not counting my chickens before they hatch, but this
election couldn't be won without @KarlRove. Genius.
Expand

Ali A. Akbar @ali   4h
This is going to be an interesting month for my personal life. Lots of
flux. Gonna ride it!
Expand   ← Reply   ⟲ Retweet   ★ Favorite

In an interesting sidebar, Shuler noted that, perhaps, someone in Germany is writing a book about Rove and Akbar.

On Sept. 5, 2012, Shuler posted:

It all started yesterday morning when I checked my blog statistics and noticed a visitor to Legal Schnauzer from someone at Holtzbrinck Publishing in New York. They arrived at my blog

by conducting keyword searches on "Karl Rove gay" and "Rove's lover is Ali Akbar." It seemed something potentially juicy was going on, and I wasn't about to let it slip unnoticed.

My first thought was, "Who in the heck is Holtzbrinck Publishing?" I had never heard of them, so I was amazed to discover, via a Google search, that this is a big-time outfit. The Georg Von Holtzbrinck Publishing Group, it turns out, is based in Stuttgart, Germany, and has published works by Ernest Hemingway, John Updike, Agatha Christie and other literary heavyweights. It also publishes international magazines, such as **Nature** and **Scientific American,** and now owns Macmillan Publishers.

As for me, I have no idea who was viewing my blog at Holtzbrinck Publishing. It might have been the CEO; it might have been a janitor with too much time on his hands. When the person first appeared on my blog stats, the visit was for a little more than five minutes. By the time, I noticed them again in the afternoon, the visit

time was for more than four hours. I sent an
update to Bill Schmalfeldt and he responded
with a new post titled "Someone Is Really,
REALLY Interested in Al Akbar and Karl Rove."

Before I start drowning in my own self
importance, it's only fair to point out that my
blog stats do not prove that someone at
Holtzbrinck was reading **Legal Schnauzer** for
a full four hours. It's possible that someone
discovered my blog, read for a while, and then
left it on the screen for much of the day while
doing other things. But this is my blog, and I **am**
self important, so we are going to assume it was
the CEO or a high-level editor who was reading
my posts the entire time--enraptured by every
word.

That leads to this obvious question: Is someone
floating a book proposal about Karl Rove and
Ali Akbar--and is Holtzbrinck interested enough
to be researching the subject?

Of course, we also have this question: Did a
supply clerk at Holtzbrinck hear about the

Rove/Akbar affair and decide to while away the hours on a slow work day, the Tuesday after Labor Day, by perusing a strange blog in far-off Alabama?

I like the first scenario better, so that's what we'll go with.

7 WITH THE EMPHASIS ON THE FORMER

Just what is this "Vice & Victory Agency" that Akbar helped create? If one goes to the website, all one sees is a logo. Just a logo. Click the logo? You're directed to a logo.

Contact v@viceandvictory.com
Copyright © 2012 Vice and Victory Agency, LLC.
All Rights Reserved.

No, if one wishes to learn more about "Vice & Victory," one has to dig. We found a website that shows, up to whenever the site was last updated, the websites that V&V has created. In the slideshow, we've included a graphic to show you which of the many websites are still doing business.

Here's a hint. Not many.

However, Vice & Victory seems to be the face that

Akbar wants most to project to the public. On their Facebook page, one will find no mention of Akbar's having been arrested and indicted for stealing items from a Fort Worth woman, then breaking into a van, stealing a debit card and trying to use it in 2007.

The Facebook page does mention a big party way down yonder in Texas where Karl Rove indicated he would attend. This would be the same Karl Rove who demanded that Zazzle remove an item from the author's tore that pictured Akbar wearing an Obama mask, waving $20 bills at whoever was taking the picture, which the flash indicates came from below Akbar... about belt level. According to what we can determine from US Copyright Law, the only way Rove can claim the intellectual property rights he claimed to have Zazzle remove the image would be if he claims he took, and therefore owns the picture. We've attempted to contact Mr. Rove to determine if he took the photo and what he was doing with a cell phone camera at Mr. Akbar's belt level, but there has been no response. No response from Mr. Akbar either, who continues to have this writer blocked from his Twitter feed.

Speaking of Twitter, Vice & Victory also has a Twitter account. It doesn't get used much. The original three followers are Aaron Marks, John Dennis Pedrie and Mr. Akbar, who are also listed as the directors of the National Bloggers Club., Inc. That's the offshoot from Vice & Victory that claimed 501(c)(3) status until this reporter and others contacted the IRS and learned they had never filed the requisite papers to claim that tax-exempt distinction.

So, what is Vice & Victory up to these days?

Hard to tell. Their website just shows a logo.

Akbar still refuses to answer any questions about how he got to where he is without a little help from well-placed friends. He still refuses to answer any questions about how Karl Rove can claim his image as "intellectual property." But he does have time to sit and complain back and forth with his sycophants about what a meanie the author is. Note, they never really mention him by his Twitter handle or by name, and they rarely use the "@" symbol when referring to him, because that way he'd be notified.

Instead, they whisper among themselves like bad little boys in the back of the classroom of a strict teacher.

Rick Mathews @Left_In_PEI

@liberalgrouch one of the biggest LIBERAL homophobes on Twitter

Ali A. Akbar @ali

@Left_In_PEI yeah. I've noticed that. I've had a lot of Lib friends give me their prayers and thoughts. He's so irrelevant it hurts. :)

*Odd thing. His blog has been anything **but** homophobic. In fact, he quite clearly states that he detests closeted gay people in positions of power who use their positions to keep other gay people from claiming the rights given in the Constitution to every other American. That's **homophobic**?*

Joe Brooks @joebrooks

@Stranahan RonB and OR seem to Tweet Burst often. I'd also consider what LG does to @ali a TweetBurst, 300 unsolicited mentions in 2 weeks.

Rick Mathews @Left_In_PEI

@ali An old guy trying to make a name for himself using the most ridiculous hyperbole..Bottom line is u are where you are, no crime in that

Ali A. Akbar @ali

*@**Left_In_PEI** indeed. His obsession with my sexuality and death is stalkerish. Dangerous even. Oh well, these are his twilight years.*

Someone seems to think quite highly of himself, does he not? "Obsessed with his death?" In his blog, the author has tried to warn Akbar what happens to young, naive gay men when their powerful "daddies" no longer have any use for them.

And if pointing out hypocrisy makes a person "homophobic", then someone has redefined the word without telling the rest of us.

LG is "The Liberal Grouch." And if Mr. Akbar would deign to be questioned like a commoner, there would be no need for "unsolicited mentions." And if "LG" is so irrelevant, who is counting the number of his Tweets, and why is that number important?

"LG" started out by asking Akbar to prove his organizations 501(c)(3) status. Worst thing to do to a good investigative reporter? Ignore him or her. The cover-up is always worse than the crime.

ALI AKBAR, VICE AND VICTORY AGENCY

CEO

Ali A. Akbar, CEO of Vice and Victory Agency -- a firm specializing in digital media political marketing as well as general public affairs and coalition-building.

Formerly with the firm Republic Modern, Ali has lead the way in implementing private-sector digital marketing strategies into the political new media field. He has been at the forefront of the blogger relations sector, coordinating with the most of the influential writers and activists to the benefit of the conservative movement and campaigns. He was among the first to call for an end to proprietary content management systems and for new media firms to bring designers and developers in-house.

Never missing a moment to buck the status quo, Ali was one of the first of a handful of National Tax Day Tea Party coordinators in February of 2009, building much of the technical infrastructure that led to the most successful protest in American history, with at least 1.2 million people attending in 81 cities.

Recently, Ali, with some of the most prominent bloggers on the right-of-center launched the National Bloggers Club, a loose-association providing bloggers with tangible resources like free photo identification badges, access to organizations and campaigns, and is building an online repository for additional digital assets.

His work has been seen on virtually every major network and publication and his opinion pieces have appeared in the Des Moines Register, New Hampshire Union-Leader, Fox News, The Daily Caller, RedState, The Dallas Morning News, and NPR, among others.

Ali also serves as an honorary board member to several non-profits and political action committees, as well as an informal advisor to many of the national Tea Party organizations.

8 NOT A WINNER IN THE BUNCH

It seems the 2012 Presidential Election turned out pretty much the way Akbar expected it would. That is, when he was the leading force behind an all-out effort to keep Romney from getting the nomination.

This was lifted from some of his "Not Mitt Romney" material of late 2011 and early 2012.

As we have done already and will continue to do, we must use Romney's own words against him to show that he will make a weak nominee if he wins the Republican nomination. Head to head national polls taken today pitting President Obama against Romney are utterly meaningless. Romney's profound weaknesses as a general election candidate (say anything, do anything to win, no core principles, not a conservative, in the words of Erick Erickson, that we "can trust") will make him weak next fall in the face of a billion dollar Obama campaign machine We must (and we will) remind Republican primary voters of this.

We will be quick to point out when **any** of the other Republican candidates create a clear contrast with Romney's ever-changing policy positions — and we will also make it clear that Romney creates only a marginal contrast against the failed presidency of Barack Obama. After all, Romney STILL supports TARP and the wildly unpopular bailouts. If Romney were to win the nomination, these type of positions will reduce participation among activists and conservatives around the country — blocs that are crucial to the successful "Get Out the Vote" operations that result in winning swing states.

Despite all of these facts, it isn't our job to present one alternative, but rather many — in fact, any. However, after Florida (if not right before), we must rally in favor of the highest performing alternative, regardless of whom that is. Mathematically, this will likely be our only remaining path to defeating Romney for the nomination. After all, the media is focused at their own national polls, not pledged delegates. Our effort is focused and targeted.

We also must continue to educate the press. Our mission is not futile. We must fight to change the narrative that falsely paints Mitt Romney as the "inevitable nominee," with the "best chance of winning" which has been constructed by the press because the **exact opposite** is true.

As you can see, our strategy is comprehensive, but our success in defeating Mitt Romney is going to rely solely on you at this critical time. As we mentioned earlier, we will soon be launching our Iowa Virtual Phone Bank. Please watch your e-mail, as when the time comes, we will need your help to make calls to Iowa voters to remind them why they must not support Romney. Of course, if you can afford to make a generous $10, $25, $50, or even $100 donation, that would help us continue to fund our critical voter contact efforts.

Thank you for your continued support. Together, we will ensure that Mitt Romney is not the Republican nominee in 2012.

Sincerely,

Ali A. Akbar, John Hawkins and Matt Mackowiak
Co-Founders, NotMittRomney.com

Of course when it was clear Romney was going to be

the nominee, what is a poor boy to do if he wants to maintain a political career with the right wing? He became a full-throated Romney supporter.

Let's look at some of Akbar's tweets from the final days of the campaign.

Ali A. Akbar @ali   5 Nov
We must destroy the Democratic Party. Make them a permanent minority party. If that means passing a compromising bill, lets do it.
Expand

Ali A. Akbar @ali   5 Nov
We're fighting against savages. Just savages. They give a damn about you and I. It's all about winning. #war
Expand

Ali A. Akbar @ali   5 Nov
It's not even midnight, the day of decision, and Obama's frontline troops are firing. Damn the media! Damn the bias!
Expand

Ali A. Akbar @ali   5 Nov
An oldie but goodie: #TeaParty Message to Morgan Freeman: 'My Name Is Ali Akbar' amsp.ec/1Ow2kR @rsmccain #throwback
Expand

Even in the midst of an election, nothing will stop Ali Akbar from shameless self-promotion.

Ali A. Akbar @all   5 Nov
Republican Party is confident about their math. Democrats are
confident about the pollz. Facts are stubborn things...
Expand

Ali A. Akbar @all   5 Nov
This is a post-election conversation, but I want you all to know now...
@TeamRomney has changed the way campaigns do things...
forever.
Expand

Ali A. Akbar @all   5 Nov
@Orlandodanny 60 / 40 sounds about right. Maybe 57 / 43
probability.
● View conversation

Ali A. Akbar @all   5 Nov
The rewrite of history has already begun by pollsters. Worry not, I
won't let them forget. #war
Expand

Ali A. Akbar @all   5 Nov
RT @feliciasonmez: Romney's closing words drowned out by huge
cheer from crowd
Expand

Ali A. Akbar @all   5 Nov
Romney is polling 5-6 times better with election day voters than
McCain in Ohio. He only needs to actually achieve half that to win
Ohio.
Expand   ← Reply   ⟲ Retweet   ★ Favorite

Ali A. Akbar @all   5 Nov
So far, Nate Silver is wrong on #Ohio. 91.4% chance that was
awkward.
Expand

Ali A. Akbar @all   5 Nov
VA + OH + FL + x = President-elect @MittRomney
Expand

Ali A. Akbar @all   5 Nov
@MarkAg86 I am betting on CO going red, but not needed, but still
will be good.
● View conversation

Ali A. Akbar @ali   5 Nov
Deleted two tweets that had bad math. Sorry. May happen a couple
of times today.
Expand

Robert Stacy McCain @rsmccain   5 Nov
Right now, @ali is on the phone talking early vote in Ohio. He likes
the numbers.
Retweeted by Ali A. Akbar
Expand

Ali A. Akbar @ali   6 Nov
If this holds. We win OH. Falling into my model. RT @SArchibald1
Romney leading in Ohio? @MartinAtwood @ali @EWErickson
news.cincinnati.com/article/201211...
Expand

Ali A. Akbar @ali   6 Nov
Breaking: Black Panthers at the SAME Philly location as 2008 trying
to intimidate voters!!!
Expand

One "New Black Panther", seen on Fox News. No
weapons. Opening doors for people. Ooooh. Scary!

Ali A. Akbar @ali   6 Nov
@shantastik I feel the same. But data is currently proving state polls
wrong and me right.
View conversation

Ali A. Akbar @ali   6 Nov
#VoteRomney #VoteRomney #VoteRomney #VoteRomney
#VoteRomney #VoteRomney #VoteRomney #VoteRomney
#VoteRomney #VoteRomney #VoteRomney
Expand

Robert Stacy McCain @rsmccain   5 Nov
MITT'S MARGIN OF VICTORY spectator.org/archives/2012/... The
Romney campaign has a real chance to win the White House
Retweeted by Ali A. Akbar
Expand

Ali A. Akbar @ali   6 Nov

.@drewcraw We'll see. I don't have VA data yet, just stuff from folks' mouths, which I never listen to. I've been bullish on VA tho - R52.6%
💬 View conversation

Ali A. Akbar @ali   6 Nov

I make a Dem assumption that Obama won #Ohio early voters by 15%. We still are headed for a win. Data is showing it's below 15%! #Winning.
Expand

Ali A. Akbar @ali   6 Nov

It's one thing to see excited Rs, it's another thing to see depressed Ds... #Ohio is experiencing BOTH. It's like a shift X4!
Expand

Ali A. Akbar @ali   6 Nov

RT @kerpen: @ali We'll win PA.
Expand

Ali A. Akbar @ali   6 Nov

Talked to sources on the @TeamRomney campaign. They're happy.
Expand

Ali A. Akbar @ali   6 Nov

President Obama had to kill Osama Bin Laden, walk through #Sandy, and lie about #Benghazi just to run neck-and-neck in polls. Ouch.
Expand

Ali A. Akbar @ali   6 Nov

.@rsmccain and I are considering skipping the Columbus victory party and just using the hotel room as a victory HQ. Who's bringing drinks?
Expand

Ali A. Akbar @ali   6 Nov

.@TheMadHessian I think we'll still win VA and FL and OH... we need ONE more. But all numbers are running diff than we needed.
💬 View conversation

Ali A. Akbar @ali   6 Nov

Just saw Obama on TV. As @MelissaTweets would say, "He's not smiling with his eyes." Losing.
Expand

Ali A. Akbar @ali   6 Nov
"He deserves to cry. I want to see him cry." - @rsmccain on
President Obama crying.
Expand

Ali A. Akbar @ali   6 Nov
Seeing Obama shed tears. That actually made me a little sad. Also
means... he knows... he knows...
Expand

Ali A. Akbar @ali   6 Nov
Candy Crowley is reporting there are "no signs of worry" from the
Romney campaign. All smiles, all winning.
Expand   ← Reply   ⇄ Retweet   ★ Favorite

Ali A. Akbar @ali   6 Nov
.@katyabram Things look great. Right on track: Exit Polls showing
crap, Ohio GOP counties up, Dems down, MSNBC wallowing. All
great signs!
● View conversation

Ali A. Akbar @ali   6 Nov
Thinking Romney gets 52-53% of Florida when it's done (even here
in an half hour or so). Could even go up.
Expand

Ali A. Akbar @ali   6 Nov
Very encouraged and surprised by Allen's numbers. I know a lot of
people are. But someone did share encouraging #s w/ me
yesterday. #VAsen
Expand

Ali A. Akbar @ali   6 Nov
Florida is Romney Country.
Expand

Ali A. Akbar @ali   6 Nov
Obama's FL lead will be gone in 5-10 mins. Has gone from 95k up to
16k up. Wait, as I was typing. Romney now ahead!
Expand

Ali A. Akbar @ali   6 Nov
Seriously considering running for Congress in #GA12 in 2014 against
Barrow should he win. I can raise the money and I'll divide his base.
Expand

God would not POSSIBLY be so good to the author as to allow Akbar to run for Congress.

Ali A. Akbar @ali   6 Nov
Secession is something openly we talk about in Texas. And I'm damn proud of that. It's immoral the debt America is raking up.
Expand

Don't let the door hit your butt on the way out.

Ali A. Akbar @ali   6 Nov
Our President will be @BarackObama. I hope he'll consider the opposition of half the country in crafting policy during this second term.
Expand

He was against Romney before he was with him and now he's against him again.

And for all the talk about secession, a frustrated Ali tweeted out this treasonous statement the following day.

Ali A. Akbar
@ali

[Follow]

Dear China, consider invading...

 Reply ↻ Retweet ★ Favorite

3
RETWEETS

1
FAVORITE

1:22 PM - 7 Nov 12 · Embed this Tweet

Ali Akbar has never, not once, backed a candidate who won ANYTHING!

2007 -- After being arrested and convicted for breaking into a man's van and stealing, then attempting to use his debit card, first-time offender Ali Abdul Razaq Akbar was released from jail. He went to work briefly as a volunteer for the John McCain campaign (Loser #1). But he was distracted by the glamour and glitz of a young, up-and-coming maverick from Georgia named Ray McKinney, who actually won the Texas GOP Presidential Straw Poll in 2007. The Georgian beat John McCain, Sam Brownback and Rick Tancredo. That was in June. But reality hit and in November 2007, would-be President McKinney traded in his aspirations to become would-be Congressman McKinney in the 12th District of Georgia

2008 — Akbar followed McKinney to Georgia and worked his ass off for him in the GOP primary. McKinney lost (Loser #2) in the primary to John Stone, who went on to lose to incumbent Democratic Congressman John Barrow.

Humiliated but never humbled, Akbar promised McKinney he would be there for him in 2010. But then, opportunity knocked.

2009 — Tea Party candidate Rob Hoffman had outpolled and outspent and outshone the Republican nominee, Dede Scozzafava. She dropped out, making the race between Democrat Bill Owens and Independent Rob Hoffman in the contest to replace Republican John McHugh, who president Obama had tabbed to be the Secretary of the Army Owens, the Democrat, beat Hoffman (Loser #3) the Independent As a side note, Owens held on to the seat in 2010 as well.

2010 — Back to Georgia. Ray McKinney needed his help again. This time, Akbar managed to get McKinney through the Primary (despite some mischief as described by McKinney's opponent. This time, the incumbent Barrow hammered McKinney 57-43%. (Loser #4).

So much for McKinney.

Akbar headed towards the nation's capital, somehow and with no visible means of support, formed the Vice and Victory Agency with other young "new media" conservatives and took to the stump for Jonathon Snyder who lost in a landslide (Loser #5) to Alex Schriver for the position of Chairman in 2010.

Yet, buoyed by Tea Party victories in 2010, Akbar kept his head in the game. He and others — including **Bill Murphy**, who was at one time the social media director for the Romney campaign until suddenly going silent during the summer when some untoward and racist tweets of his surfaced (anybody check the ditches and culverts) — formed the National Bloggers Club, Inc., as a 501(c)3 organization to assist bloggers who were being attacked by liberals. Two problems. They never filed the papers to become a legitimate 501(c)3, so anyone making a donation to the NBC, Inc., WILL have to pay taxes on that donation. And the blogger they primarily organized to "defend" has been revealed as having lied about the reasons he was fired.

Early in the 2012 Election Season (late 2011) to be exact, Akbar was one of the co-founders of the "NotMittRomney.com" website, which we featured on the Patriot-Ombudsman yesterday.

One thing is certain. Ali Akbar has never, ever, not once, backed a winner. Anyone who listens to him, who takes his political advice, who puts any stock in anything he says, needs to understand that.

Ali Akbar
HOST ORGANIZER
Ali got his start by blogging, eventually becoming one of the most read political bloggers on MySpace. Remember, it was popular once upon a time. Recently, he returned to the blogosphere, although many would say he never left. Ali is the Vice President of Digital Strategy with Vice and Victory Agency, LLC, a firm specializing in political marketing on the digital medium as well as general public affairs and coalition building. He is the Publisher of Tea Party Brew, published by the content arm of his operation, Pundit Syndication. He is also a contributor to Andrew Brietbart's BigJournalism.com and Technorati.com—one of the most trafficked sites in North America. Never missing a moment to fight the establishment, he was one of the first few National Tax Day Tea Party coordinators in February of 2009, building much of the technical infrastructure that led to the most successful protest in American history—with at least 1.2 million people attending in 81 cities organically. His work has been seen on every major network and publication and his opinion pieces have appeared on well known publications and blogs, including The Daily Caller, PBS, Fox News, GBTV, RedState, The Dallas Morning News, and NPR. He tweets @ali.

Let's review further scoops of fine, fertile soil shoveled from Larry Sinclair's exhaustive nine-month-long investigation into the activities of Ali Akbar and the group known as the National Bloggers' Club,.

When you look at the names of those who are listed as sponsors of Blog Bash at CPAC 2012, you would think that the event was a sincere conservative effort but what you don't immediately see is the Host organizers are also the top named sponsors of the event. Melissa I love Bloggers is none other than Melissa Clouthier an

*associate of Ali Akbar who is into promoting herself and
her skills at attacking people on Twitter.*

Let's take a look at Ms. Clouthier, shall we? For one
thing, her blog, MelissaBlogs.com, was designed by
Akbar's Vice & Victory agency.

© 2005 - 2012 **Dr. Melissa Clouthier**
Graphic design by **Vice & Victory**
Developed and maintained by **DJS Consulting**
Powered by **WordPress 3.4.2**

Her most recent post is a spot-on prediction of the
presidential election outcome.

*The media, left, and poll watchers seem 84% convinced
that Barack Obama is a shoe-in. Or, it's tied 48-48. 47-
47. The models have Obama running away with the
electoral college.*

*In my bones, I don't believe this. Some states are going to
be lost, no doubt. But this guaranteed result? Bah.*

Vote. I feel good about my Mitt vote and you should, too.

Then, we have Tabitha Hale, listed in Sinclair's story as
being "director of New Media" at the Franklin Center.

(Odd how they haven't updated their site since the election.) We find it downright shocking that a director of "New Media" would not respond to a request from a fellow-conservative in the New Media (Sinclair), so we tried *our* hand at it.

Bill Schmalfeldt

To: tabitha.hale@franklincenterhq.org
Request for information

November 8, 2012 9:26 AM

Hi there, Ms. Hale.

I see you are listed as director of New Media for the Franklin Center. I saw a story by Larry Sinclair this morning on his website, and I wanted to give you a chance to set the record straight.

Was the Franklin Center, in fact, a sponsor of Blog Bash at any time? You are listed as a sponsor, but Mr. Sinclair says all attempts at communication with you have been fruitless. I thought I'd take a shot at it to see if I could get an official response.

Thanks for your time!

Bill Schmalfeldt
Editor
The Patriot-Ombudsman

Now, let's examine **"Donation Control."** Sinclair says this…

DonationControl.com is another Akbar founded and operated entity which has come under scrutiny which is part of Three Group LLC doing business in the State of PA.

Let's lift the hood and take a looksee.

Here's the top part of the landing page.

Nice. Smooth. Serious looking Republican candidate.
Let's see what we get when we try to sign up for one of
their free accounts.

OK, we filled out the info, gave some personal info.
They asked us how we wished to be paid, but only gave
one method… electronic transfer of funds… which
means we have to send them a fax of a voided check.
WITH MY BANK ACCOUNT NUMBER ON IT!!!

WHAT? You can't pay me through Pay Pal like a REPUTABLE donation service??? We're going to give my bank account number to a convicted debit card fraudster? Uh, no!

Let's take a closer look at this thing and find out for sure who's behind it.

When you hit "Donation Control" it takes you to a link for http://www.getmissioncontrol.com/donation-control/ — at the bottom of the home page, you see that Donation Control is a proud part of "Mission Control." Click that link.

UNPRECEDENTED VICTORIES??? HOORAY!

Well, out of the 15 elections highlighted here, 9 were losers.

Everything You Need to Win.

Dozens of campaigns, candidates, organizations, and political groups have used our powerful election software to build unprecedented victories.

Sign up today for our 30-day free no obligation trials!

Selected Past and Present Clients

UNPRECEDENTED VICTORIES??? HOORAY!

Let's look at some of these "victories. Yeah, McDonnell won his gubernatorial election. Charlie Baker had his butt handed to him by Patrick Deval, 48-42% in the Mass. Gubernatorial election in 2010. Danny Tarkanian, now THERE'S a success story. He ran for state senate in Nevada in 2004, lost 54-46%. Lost a race for Nevada Secretary of State in 2006, 48-40%. Came in 3rd among Republicans in the 2010 GOP primary. And just lost in his race for Congress in the new Nevada 4th District, 50-42%. (Somebody buy this guy a hint?) Toomey won his race for Senate. But Tom Campbell got HAMMERED by Carly Fiorina in the 2010 California GOP Senatorial Primary, 56-21%. Mariannette Miller-Meeks got beat TWICE by Iowa Congressman David Loebsack, once in 2008, again in 2010. Jim Gerlach was successful in his Pennsylvania house race. Michigan Congressman Fred Upton kept his seat. Jeff Perry HAD been in the Congress since 2003. Then he signed up with Mission Control and got beat in 2010. Tim Murphy kept his seat. Tom Wesley was beaten senseless 52-47% in his 2010 Mass. congressional run. Kathleen Donovan IS the Bergen County, NJ, Executive! You would think Sean Bielat would be tired of being beaten like a drum. Barney Frank beat him in 2010, Joe Kennedy III whalloped him the other day. Bill Hudak got the bottom of the boot from voters in 2010m and Jon Golnik got Niki Tsognas' high heel in the eye in 2010, he got the other heel in the other eye this year.

But who runs "Mission Control?"

THAT would be "The Three Group." And who are THEY? And didn't Mr. Sinclair's story say that Ali Akbar founded this group?

Well, that might not be quite true. But we know who *was* the CEO from 2007 until earlier this year.

Aaron Marks

Senior Marketing & Communications Specialist at RJ Lee Group

Greater Pittsburgh Area | Online Media

Previous   Three Group, LLC, Engage, LLC

Education   BS, Business Administration at Carnegie Mellon University

Send InMail ▾

147
connections

WHO WE ARE

Founded in 2005, Three Group is a Pittsburgh-based interactive, new media, and software development firm that specializes in building political technology solutions. Our team's vast experience allows us to build bold, innovative solutions for our clients.

We believe that technology plays a fundamental role in shaping our lives. When used properly, technology can not only enhance an organization's efforts, but in many cases it can be the defining factor. It is Three Group's fundamental belief that every client's demands are unique. As a result we work with our clients through the entire design and development process to ensure that the solution we provide is custom-tailored to meet their needs while exceeding their expectations.

Today's best media has an emphasis on modern, advanced design. We present powerful, effective solutions that meet today's rigorous standards head on.

Who also happens to be…

Who also happens to be…

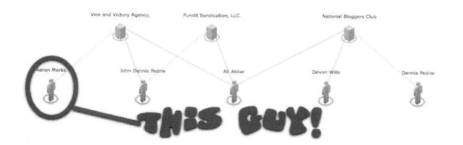

> **"Oh, what a tangled web we weave when first we practice to deceive!"**

OK, so we know that any money you try to gather from Donation Control needs to have a direct deposit account verified by a check sent to Aaron Marks' Three Group, and Aaron Marks is a partner of Ali Akbar, and Ali Akbar is a convicted Debit Card Fraud.

So, the question we pose to conservatives who ignore our warnings and posts about Akbar's criminal background is this:

Why would you willingly, with eyes wide open, give your credit card info and bank account numbers to a man convicted of breaking into someone's truck and stealing his debit card? What in God's name are you thinking? Do you believe the documents you've seen in our blogs and this book are fabricated? Do you think we're "out to get" this skeezy little ex-con who is stealing YOUR money – not ours?

And how can you trust someone to manage the funds of a club or a corporation, when he has proven to be incapable of managing his OWN funds?

Breitbart Unmasked penned this blog post on June 21, 2012:

It is amazing sometimes to witness the hilarity that goes on in blog wars. In the case of Ali Akbar, convicted felon, he now runs a supposed non profit called the National Bloggers Club which has been raising boatloads of cash off of various right wing conservative bloggers and wealthy businessmen such as Foster Friess. The effort of course seems hollow when you look at the past of Ali Akbar. Following up on earlier stories on BU about him, BU ran across a recent court filing for eviction and forcible entry and detainer at one of the apartments he lived at in Savannah Georgia. It seems that Ali had trouble paying his bills and or rent and was forcibly evicted from this property due to non-payment. Yet, here is he today raising money and telling people that he can manage their money better than he could manage his own. Couple that with recent trips to Las Vegas to attend the Right Online conference, as well as trips back and forth to D.C. to meet with big shot donors and politicians makes one wonder if he really is managing "other peoples money" as well as he managed his own? There is of course that nagging question of whether or not the National Bloggers Club has actually obtained that 501c designation from the IRS, or if its still pending while he continues to tell donors and other elites that all of their money that they donate is tax deductible. But whether it is or not at this point isn't really the question as I am sure at some point they will obtain their tax status. In the mean time the question I have to ask myself is whether or not Mr. Akbar is capable of managing other peoples money, because it is quite clear he wasn't managing his own money in the recent past.

Of course this goes without saying that most of these right wing conservatives who have been out bashing others such as Brett Kimberlin have pretty much scammed other people out of money as in the recent article on BU concerning Lee Stranahan. I also make note of other people in this National Bloggers Club mix who either skipped out on paying their bills by filing Chapter 7 bankruptcy while still having a job, or those who ran scams and or ripped people off such as Lee Stranahan and his Learning Digital Fusion scam that he ran back in 2004, and coupled with Mr. Akbar's convictions for credit card fraud, burglary and theft, makes this National Bloggers Club stink to high heaven in my opinion. It seems that the people mixed into this club have a number of financial problems in their past, and none of them truly want to own up to it. They would prefer to just keep it all dark and secret while going out begging for money to help them relocate to a new home, or go to Las Vegas for a good time, or even to travel and meet and greet power brokers, all I might add off the backs of hard working conservatives who have been led down a false path or narrative that was created just so they could donate money to this elitist club, and all so those that are a part of the inner circle could have fun off of the backs of those conservatives.

I recently read some comments on another blog about how people should be questioning the leadership of The National Bloggers Club, and then ran across a comment that claimed that Foster Friess the wealthy billionaire who initially bankrolled the club was made aware of Mr. Akbar's past convictions and seemingly had no problem with it. However it is a problem, and because he failed to disclose these issues of Mr. Akbar to the membership and those who were asked to fund this little attack dog club venture, questions are now being raised on whether this club can even exist in its present form or with the current head of the club which is Ali A. Akbar.

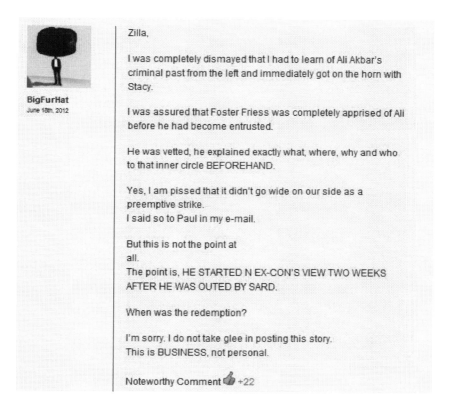

Zilla,

I was completely dismayed that I had to learn of Ali Akbar's criminal past from the left and immediately got on the horn with Stacy.

BigFurHat
June 18th, 2012

I was assured that Foster Friess was completely apprised of Ali before he had become entrusted.

He was vetted, he explained exactly what, where, why and who to that inner circle BEFOREHAND.

Yes, I am pissed that it didn't go wide on our side as a preemptive strike.
I said so to Paul in my e-mail.

But this is not the point at all.
The point is, HE STARTED N EX-CON'S VIEW TWO WEEKS AFTER HE WAS OUTED BY SARD.

When was the redemption?

I'm sorry. I do not take glee in posting this story.
This is BUSINESS, not personal.

Noteworthy Comment 👍 +22

I think it is amazing that the elites or major financial backers of the National Bloggers Club would cover up such issues or fail to disclose these past criminal issues with Mr. Akbar to the members and or future

donors. It is almost like saying they needed to cover

it up because they had this guy who seemed to be

great on the surface for their operations against

democrats, but because he had this twisted past

they needed to hush it up from everyone else so

they could make a quick run down to the well and

grab the money fast. That is part and parcel of the

elites in the conservative movement, which is hush

up the past while fleecing the sheep in the future.

Because at the end of the day its all about the

dollars while the manufactured cause to raise it is

left on the cutting room floor. I question just how

long this operation can go on without a house

cleaning. But even if a housecleaning takes place

one would venture to query why one was needed so

early into the process of building this operation? Are

conservatives so eager to get their messages out

that quality over quantity makes no difference? I

shudder to think what other revelations will be forthcoming. However until that day arrives it is open season on the sheep that donate to their manufactured causes, and buyer beware is all I can think of to say about it. The only real question now is how long will it take to clean house at the National Bloggers Club? Or maybe the question should be: should the donors demand a housecleaning of their own before they continue to donate to others who claim they can manage donor money better than they can manage their own?

9 THE DEFINITION OF INSANITY

So, what does Akbar want? What is he after, other than power and money given to him by suckers? What motivates this little Sammy Davis Jr.-looking fraud?

Well, before you could point and shout "SCOREBOARD: at President Obama's 3-million vote margin (larger than Bush's in 2004) and his 336-206 Electoral Vote victory (topped only by his 365-173 drubbing of John McCain in 2008, more than George W. Bush "I have political capital. I am going to spend it" in EITHER of his elections), Akbar is calling on the Speaker of the House to do the exact same thing that led to Obama's victory and to the Democratic pickups in the House and Senate.

Delay. Stall. Obstruct.

In his "Viral Read" blog (even his blog name is filled with ego and hubris), Akbar writes (and we deconstruct):

Speaker Boehner,

America is standing on a stool with a noose around her neck. And Obama is kicking the stool. For the next two years, **you're the only man who can stop him**.

(This proposes the failed meme that Obama is trying to kill the United States. A Tea Party/Wingnut meme the voters rejected.)

We have to spend less.

This is not an abstract concept. This is not a political statement. This isn't last time.

This is math. It's reality. To survive as a free and independent nation, the federal government needs its receipts to exceed its expenditures.

Politics is the art of compromise. Fine. Stop compromising on the Democrats' terms.

(To Wingnut/Tea Party people, "compromise" means "do it our way.)

Negotiations begin at a 5% spending cut across the board. The bare minimum you can accept is a balanced budget.

(Reminder. SCOREBOARD!)

You were elected to enact your campaign promises to repeal Obamacare and cut federal spending.

(The people WANT Obamacare. They don't love ALL of it, but they want it. They voted for it. Again... SCOREBOARD!)

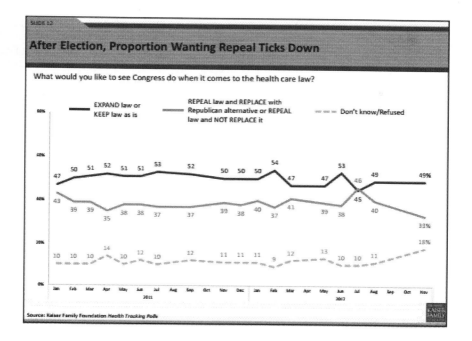

Do what you promised. Repealing Obamacare is a proven political winner.

(Classic deluded thinking. Just like Romney's not releasing his tax returns was a proven political winner.)

As it gets implemented – and as doctors start closing their offices – there will be a new outcry against it.

(Doctors will not start closing their offices. Those that do don't deserve a patient's trust.)

Don't back down. Make your case to the American people. Then hold the line, even if it means your job.

(And it will.)

This is bigger than you, bigger than your seat and your career. It's bigger than your Speakership. It's bigger than Congress.

(It's even bigger than the twice-declared will of a majority of the voters.)

Our debt has become a matter of national security. If America falls from power, other nations, including America's enemies, will quickly fill that void. If you fail, you will have endangered billions of people.

(Remember a fellow, what was his name? Ah! Dick Cheney? You supported him? Said "deficits don't matter?" At least, they didn't with a Republican in the White House.)

The fiscal cliff is right in front of us.

(The fiscal curb.)

After that, we'll hit the debt ceiling again. If you let Obama spend his way past those problems, you're feeding the monster and just putting him off for another day.

(Bush raised the debt ceiling 7 times. Reagan did it 18 times. Somehow, the nation endured.)

Be brave! Summon the courage to call Obama's bluff. Appeal to America's better angels. Tell them to sacrifice a little like their parents did for them.

(As long as those sacrifices don't involve making rich people pay any more in taxes?)

You are the man who must make it happen. For the next two years, you're all we've got.

Call it luck. Call it fate. Call it karma. Circumstances are going to make a hero or a villain out of you.

(Too late. We all know what Boehner is.)

You'll be remembered in the history books as the man who let disaster happen or the one who pulled America back from the brink. Your choice.

(Creating strawmen is your specialty, it seems.)

Times are hard. Your caucus, in addition to the results of the election, present a complicated political problem. We know this.

If you make your stand for America's future, you may be surprised by the strength behind you.

(Or, at how quickly the GOP loses its House majority in 2014.)

So. Akbar thinks his horrible misreading of the election results, like his horrible misreading of the pre-election tea leaves, gives him the credibility to tell the Speaker of the House of Representatives what to do. We do hope he will let us know how that works out.

But even more than his hatred of debt and deficits, there is one other thing (other than lust for money, scotch and anonymous sex hookups) that motivates him.

One thing, a deep and abiding – and baffling – hatred of Brett Kimberlin. From a letter posted on Akbar's Facebook account on June 8, just days after Akbar's story broke online.

Dear Brett Kimberlin,

Your harassment of liberal and conservative bloggers exposing your violent and racist prompted my involvement. Veteran journalist Robert Stacy McCain called me in a panic. He and his family needed to be relocated, he asked me "where are you?" I simply replied, "I'll be out the door in 15 minutes". When a prominent member of our board, Michelle Malkin, asked what our National Bloggers Club would do to step up and protect our members, we leapt into action. I supported Lee Stranahan's call for a "Everyone Blog about Brett Kimberlin Day."

When I heard Aaron Walker and his wife were unemployed, I not only raised funds to relieve his strife but chipped in myself. When pro bono lawyers need to be found, I coordinated.

You're a convicted domestic terrorist and filing frivolous lawsuits against members of the media and bloggers who would dare speak to your past. And when that happens the same online accounts, the same characters including Neal Rauhauser attack in very real, very violent ways.

You're aware too. Two bloggers have had dangerous falsified SWAT calls on their families.

They've managed to harass Aaron and his wife's employer until they were let go. My mother's home address, pictures of her home, her last names from previous manages, my relatives, including my Great Aunt and second cousin have been listed all over the internet and tweeted to anyone who will listen. Minions are being incited to commit violence and unlawful behavior against my family. My mugshot is on fringe websites. Now, they're going after another blogger, Jeff, because he dared offered free space on his website's sidebar to raise relief funds for Aaron and others who are being attacked by your cyber-bullies.

Worse, you're these sympathizers of yours are coming after me with more. Alleging drug use, federal crimes, voter fraud and sexual promiscuity. Now, I comfort my strong mother's tears as she watches your cohorts tear apart my life. Does it end Brett? Will it stop?

Now yes, I had a several month stint around the time I turned 21 where I was drinking, partying, and did some very stupid things. I dropped out of bible college, left the ministry, dropped out of the

University of North Texas and was estranged from my family. I largely hurt myself, embarrassed my mother. I've never hidden this and on a near daily basis, I'm reminded of how it has hindered my future. Because of those childish few months and 2 cases that ended up being tried a year apart, I cannot do everything people of my age can do. I carry baggage that'll follow me. I understand all of this.

I've never been violent. I've never stolen from an individual. I don't lie. I'm the same man who supports Meals on Wheels in north Texas, who donated over 1 ton of food to St. Mary's in Savannah over the past two years, who rallied with some of my readers to raise $750 to feed the homeless in Boston when Occupy protests interrupted their food drive, who challenged Morgan Freeman and Soledad O'Brien when they screamed racism about my political ideology. I was a part of that small skeleton crew (along with Eric Odom, Amy Kremer, Jenny Beth Martin, and two dozen others) that ran TaxDayTeaParty.com and organized 81 cities for some of the first Tea Party rallies. I am Ali A. Akbar.

You, well you blew up a man's body part. He committed suicide because of you. Have some shame. This is true evil.

You've probably destroyed part of my career -- maybe all of it. In this time though, my friends have been enduring. The ACLJ has rush to the defense of bloggers everywhere. Prominent commentators and members of Congress have decided to associate themselves with this cause.

When someone -- anyone calls who has been wronged by yourself, Neal Rauhauser and/or these anonymous hackers -- I'll rush to their aid if they'll have me. It's my calling.

I'm a believer (and it absolves me of nothing I've done here on this earth -- it's not my get-out-of-jail free card). I do however have a knowing and a love you choose to not understand. And it is this love, this dedicated love that I commit to chase this cause to its end.

I've been asked several times, how does this end? **With you in jail.**

And now that the election is over, and Akbar has ruined his OWN career by backing yet another losing candidate? What does he want now?

We will admit to a moment of hope in the first day or two after President Obama beat Mitt Romney.

For a minute there, we thought Ali Akbar had learned a political lesson from his humiliation last Tuesday. we thought that maybe, perhaps, a light had gone on in that dim little cavern of a cranium that isn't concerned with meeting new "chill buds" or fleecing the flock for

moolah. Some of his tweets even had me thinking that there might be, maybe, a sincere bone in his scrawny, Sammy Davis Junior-looking body.

But we were wrong. We committed the sin of thinking there might be a soul in that underfed frame.

I was depressed. We had just lost the most important election of our lifetime and I wasn't going to be chipper or be one of the commentators telling people to pick themselves up. **This isn't a game**. I don't do this purely for profit. I convinced people to sacrifice a lot—I've sacrificed so much over these past two years.

A Twitter follower turned friend explained to me that he and several others looked to me for leadership. I was his "big brother." It was humbling and made me proud of the work I've done. I had been weeping for my country, my future, my loss; But this was no time for a further deficit of leadership.

And then I lept into fury...

The hubris! The EGO! "THEY LOOK TO ME FOR LEADERSHIP?" WHO? WHO IN GOD'S NAME WITH HALF A BRAIN IN HIS OR HER SKULL WOULD LOOK TO A SKEEZY EX CON, ADEBIT CARD FRAUDSTER, for LEADERSHIP???

So. Akbar LEAPED into a FURIOUS FURY OF ANGER AND FURY! (There's no such word as *"lept."* *"Leapt"* is acceptable in some circles, but the preferred past tense of *"leap"* is *"leaped."*)

In other words, he started tweeting like a wounded weasel.

Really. And we're just going to sit here and let you do that? You're going to take Black mothers and Black children AWAY from us? You're going to shut down Liberal media? We thought you morons were AGAINST the Fairness Act.

Besides… LIBERAL MEDIA??? Son, that dog just don't hunt. Here's a list of things that do not exist.

Santa Claus
The Easter Bunny
The Tooth Fairy
Honesty in the New Conservative Media
Karl Rove's Subscription to "Hustler"
and
THE LIBERAL MEDIA

It's a myth, son! There AIN'T no such animal! The "media" is owned, lock-stock-and-barrel by CORPORATIONS that do NOT have a "liberal" agenda! The only "agenda" you will find in the so-called "liberal media" is LUST FOR RATINGS! It's not NEWS, Akbar! It's "Keeping Eyeballs on the Screen!"

And what are you bitching about? You HAVE your own network. When the other networks called Ohio for

Obama, Karl Rove (remember him, his scent, his taste, Ali?) PERSONALLY kept Fox News from making the announcement because HE SAID IT COULD NOT BE POSSIBLE!!! Are you that BLIND? That STUPID?

No. WE don't think you are. We think you are dishonest. Not stupid.

More of your angry Tweets of Fury.

Ali A. Akbar @ali — Follow

Democrats, we're going to "O'Keefe" your unions and disban them after we expose bullying, corruption and illegal activities.

7 Nov 12 — Reply Retweet Favorite

Ali A. Akbar @ali — Follow

We have to blow the Democrats' coalition up. Pick up Reagan's three-legged stool and just start breaking shit.

7 Nov 12 — Reply Retweet Favorite

Ali A. Akbar @ali — Follow

We should pass a pro-woman specific bill out of the House every month for the next 2 yrs. Lets take women from them. Let them hear we care.

7 Nov 12 — Reply Retweet Favorite

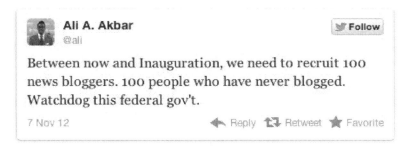

Ali A. Akbar @ali — Follow

Between now and Inauguration, we need to recruit 100 news bloggers. 100 people who have never blogged. Watchdog this federal gov't.

7 Nov 12 — Reply Retweet Favorite

Well, for one thing, the word is "disband." Not "disban." And for another thing, you're promising to do more of the same shit that cost you THIS election, only faster and harder? The definition of Insanity, Akbar? Doing the same thing that failed over and over and over again, expecting different results?

This list of yours? You will do no such thing. You will bitch and whine and it will be all for nothing because THE PEOPLE HAVE SPOKEN!

Democracy's a bitch, ain't it just?

And look at the photo at the beginning of this chapter. See? There is the crux of your problem. THE PEOPLE HATE THE FACT THAT THE REPUBLICANS DID NOT COOPERATE WITH OBAMA!!! By a margin of 3-million popular votes, AMERICA SAID THEY WANT OBAMA'S AGENDA!

Congress? Republicans have control of the House for one reason. Gerrymandering. Indeed, more than *half-a-million* more Americans voted for Democratic House candidates than for Republicans House candidates. It's the truth, Akbar. You once had a nodding acquaintance with it. Numbers don't lie. More people voted for DEMOCRATS than REPUBLICANS and that is a FACT!

But you are going to work with your fellow movement conservative criminals to thwart the will of the majority? You've started a new Facebook page to that effect? Good luck with that, and we'll see you in 2014. But first, we think every conservative reading these words needs to ask you a question, Akbar.

"What did you do with the money we donated to the National Bloggers Club?"

"Where is that full accounting you said we would get?"

WHAT DID YOU DO WITH THEIR MONEY, AKBAR?

How much have you raised, how much was spent on the stated purpose of the National Bloggers Club, whatever that was, and how much was spent to keep you in anonymous boy sex and cigarettes for Bobby McCain.

PEOPLE ARE LOOKING TO YOU FOR LEADERSHIP, YOU SKEEZY LITTLE CROOK? DON'T THEY DESERVE ANSWERS?

And for those of you who were stupid enough to join up with Akbar on his little Facebook party? You deserve to be fleeced for every cent Akbar can get out of your bank accounts. He's not ripping off liberals and independents, you dumbasses. CONSERVATIVES are HIS ATM! And his lies are the illegally-obtained DEBIT CARD he got when he BROKE INTO YOUR CHILDLIKE TRUST in him. So join his little Facebook page. "Like" him. LOOK TO HIM FOR LEADERSHIP! And when he needs your money? GIVE IT TO HIM LIKE THE STUPID, DELUDED SHEEP YOU ARE!

He'll spend it wisely. That subscription to Grindr ain't *free*, ya know!

10 AND IT'S MORE THAN JUST AKBAR

Of course, it's not just Ali Akbar that conservatives should be concerned about. There are those who benefit from his largesse. The lackey, lickspittles who hang around Akbar and tell him how great and smart he is. Akbar keeps them in beer and cigarette money, and damned if they are going to say or do anything to disrupt the gravy train.

Lead among the lickspittle lackeys is the loathsome Robert Stacy McCain, who blogs under the title "The Other McCain."

In a November 2, 2012, post directed at notorious right wing blogger, Larry Sinclair, blasting him for seeking truth where lies dwell, McCain takes his "fellow conservative" to task for daring to question Akbar.

Bill Schmalfeldt is jumping up and down yelling about a bunch of insanity you spouted on your show last night, which I don't have time to sort through. I'm covering a presidential campaign, having traveled to Ohio at considerable expense, a trip I could not have made without the assistance of Ali Akbar.

Schmalfeldt's motives for attacking me and Ali are obvious enough — Schmalfeldt is a liberal and an ally of Neal Rauhauser — but your motives in abetting this malicious defamation puzzle me. This is nothing more than a distraction, and I have no alternative but to suppose that its purpose is the same as its effect, that you (and Schmalfeldt, et al.) are deliberately endeavoring to distract Ali and me from the work we are doing.

And hey, Larry, "bloviating blowhard ... Michelle Malkin"? Good luck with the rest of your life, sir. As I told someone several weeks ago, if you think you're going to throw Ali Akbar under your bus, I've got news for you: Your bus ain't big enough. Ali's valuable services to the conservative cause are so widely known, by so many estimable people in the conservative movement, that these vile falsehoods you are promoting cannot really harm him, even if they hurt him. Only a sadistic personality could take pleasure in smearing someone under such circumstances, and your wickedness is therefore self-evident.

In September, I reached out to you because I believed you were a good person who had somehow been manipulated into mistakenly attacking me. What you have done now convinces me that I must have misjudged the situation, and that you have become an active and willing agent of evil. Repent before it is too late.

McCain has, as of this date, written six columns about how irrelevant I am.

There is, of course, the eminently mockable Aaron Walker who blogs under the name of Aaron Worthing on a blog called "Allergic 2 Bull" which is an odd name to call a blog where that is all one seems to be capable of slinging. There is very little, if any, truth to be found there.

But we have enjoyed mocking him for his weepy tales of losing his job because of the evil terror of Brett Kimberlin who is working for social justice after serving time for a crime committed four decades ago. In fact, he did not lose his job because of terrorist threats. We exposed that lie in a blog post you can find on The Patriot-Ombudsman, in a series you can find here.

http://patriot-ombudsman.com/category/scoundrels-and-crooks/aaron-walker-scoundrels-and-crooks

Enjoy that on your own time. Here's a piece we wrote for the wonderful blog "Borderless News and Views" in which we mock the mockable. Published Sept. 10, 2012, it is called:

ERRIN' WORTHING FINDS OWN BUTTCRACK, EVERYONE SMILES!

"I had to use both o' me hands to do it," said noted former lawyer Erring Wortheringtonshireham Walker, "but I found me ass crack! Aye, it was a long search, but I finally found whar the good lord split me!

There was much celebrating. "It's more than we ever expected of the lad," Mayor Stran Lyinghham said.

IN OTHER NEWS

Neanderthal blogger and one-time lawyer for TWO jurisdictions, Aaron Walker (Worthing) revealed that

arch evil villain (he pronounces it "villy-un") Bill
Schmalfeldt once accepted a friend request from
Brett Kimberlin on his rarely used Facebook page.
"He's the Liberal Grouch! Did you know that,"
Worthing blathered to anyone who would listen as
he cranked out his latest work of art on a Royal
Typewriter hooked to a toaster that he calls "The
Internet Thing"

"This proves EVERYTHING! HE IS A KIMBERLIN
ASSOCIATE!!! IT'S RIGHT THERE ON HIS
FACEBOOK PAGE!!! AROOO! AROOOO!"

Other Kimberlin associates (because Aaron says
so) include someone who looks like a South Park
character, someone who has the same last name
as a popular line of frozen TV Dinners (which
means Kimberlin is going to freeze our bodies and
eat them later), the Zig Zag cigarette paper man,
some other guy in a hat, and , احتلابدرای پیشبرد
سکولادردموکرسای دراریان

We haven't checked, but we think that means
"Death to America." We'll just assume it does.

Walker Worthing filled out several other column inches on his blog, which ultimately means you have to give AT LEAST $50 to his "I don't want to find a real job" fund, which you can find convenient links to implanted into your forehead.

Basically it's the same warmed over blather about how Bill Schmalfeldt hates Jesus and America, too, and how he personally threatened to violate the tender, sore anal tissue of Stran Leemingham with a fence pole wrapped in barbed wire, but the clever devil worded it in such a way as to confuse us by making it NOT look like a threat, but WE know what he meant. If we leave out chunks of what he actually said, we can make him say anything we want. For instance, in his post today, Worthing Aarington actually wrote these words.

Patrick "Patterico" Frey is beating his infant son, doing his level best to threaten vile conduct and brass-knucke thuggery!

HE WROTE THESE WORDS!

Not in that ORDER of course, but it's clear what he meant! It's all in the editing.

Ever since I called the Liberal Grouch (LG) on his vile conduct (see here, here, and here) he has been doing his level best to perform brass-knuckle reputation management, beating his chest, claiming somehow that accurately quoting him and then expressing the opinion that his words amount to a threat is libel. And now he is trying to threaten the employment of Patrick "Patterico" Frey for supposedly lying about him. More Kimberlin-style thuggery from one of his associates.

But I have long made a sardonic observation about my life: I have been blessed with stupid adversaries.

You see what LG is complaining about is not only *not libelous*, but *LG has actually said it was not libel.*

But let me back up for a moment and fill in some of the holes. First, yesterday I wrote that LG had threatened Lee Stranahan with rape and that I suspected that this was why Lee was abandoning his home in Texas. He does have an infant son, after all. When he whined about my piece, I added the following update to my post

In other words:

Aaron Worthing Walker McStupid is a moron. Give him your money.

And no book about Breitbartian clods would be complete without a few paragraphs about the toothless wonder, Lee Stranahan.

A legend in his own mind, an arteest in dumbass clothing, Stranahan is the sort of person that if you look at the wrong way, he will run to Teacher and say you were picking on him. I relate this story, written by Matt Osborne, about the night Lee Stranahan sent the Howard

County, Maryland, police to my house one night, so THEY could laugh at him TOO! (You can find the original here -- http://www.osborneink.com/2012/09/lee-stranahan-calls-the-police-to-silence-a-liberal-fails.html)

Police arrived at the Maryland home of Liberal

blogger Bill Schmalfeldt, aka The Liberal Grouch,

last night just after he had finished posting a new

fundraiser for Lee Stranahan's dental work. Stranahan, who blogs for Breitbart.com, says Schmalfeldt "threatened" him by republishing address information that Stranahan had given him:

The cops see old, trembly me with my walker, my cancer survivor wife on the couch, apologizes and leaves."

And this, just MOMENTS after Lee Stranahan tweeted about a new threat on his life.

If you are threatening the life of Lee Stranahan, stop it right now.

Me, I'm glad the cops are so responsive.

The officer left, but he came back. I invited him in to look at my computer. We went through my blog and he saw that the pictures I posted of the inside of Stranahan's house are freely available

online. I did not come into anyone's house, and Stranahan sent me his address when I applied for his Bloggy Class. We looked at my Twitter stream. He saw I made NO threats to ANYONE. In fact, my blog was clear about anyone thinking about doing anything NOT doing anything because it would be BAD!

Stranahan later admitted to making the police report on Twitter:

Lee has spent the day pushing this fabricated nonsense on Twitter. He has transitioned, however, claiming now that Schmalfeldt threatened to "rape" his family. All of these "threats" are ridiculous contrivances, which are nothing new for Lee.

In June, he accused a prominent progressive Twitter user of a criminal act, even though the charge was entirely based on the secondhand word of a hoax personality enacting a smear.

In his blog, Schmalfeldt has been tracking Stranahan's long and continuing history of self-dealing: Stranahan is a lying, fabricating scam artist. He confesses a journey to conservatism that begins with Ayn Rand, so he probably thinks himself a regular Galtian superman right about now.

But Lee is actually just a punk who likes to bully people.

He has made a mistake, though, because Schmalfeldt is not intimidated. He now says that he will pursue charges against Stranahan. Despite suffering from advancing Parkinson's, Schmalfeldt remains strong and well-humored.

I am not so well-humored, because I have seen too much of this behavior from Stranahan. For example, he obsesses about random Twitter users in his blog and then deletes their comments when they set him straight. Like the rest of the wingnutosphere, his persecution narratives are just psychological projection.

Stranahan works for Breitbart.com, the same website where Chris and Dana Loesch yap about #TwitterGulag, but it is Schmalfeldt whose Twitter account has been suspended at least twice in recent months for asking right wing bloggers uncomfortable questions related to the National Bloggers Club (NBC).

While researching a related story this weekend, I confirmed a report that Stranahan also played "enforcer" with Paul Lemmen, the conservative blogger who first called foul on Ali Akbar and NBC. As Alex Brant-Zawadski reported yesterday, the NBC is a fraudulent charity, and merely the latest questionable Akbar venture.

The timing of this attempted intimidation seems suspicious. Tea Party conservatives demanded accountability from the NBC last week, and Brant-Zawadzki reported that former NBC Director Bill Murphy had become Social Media Director for the Romney campaign without ever listing his role at the NBC on his resume.

Is Stranahan acting like a mafia goon, threatening and intimidating the NBC's critics? Schmalfeldt has reportedly spurred an IRS investigation into their activities, so to me this whole story smells like obstruction of justice. Somebody wants to change the subject away from right wing criminality to imaginary liberal threats.

It's not going to work.

We decided against pursuing charges. Punishment enough, we figure, waking up every morning being Lee Stranahan.

But that did not stop him from trying to raise a few bucks off the deadly threat we made against him. And this caught the eye of perhaps the second most-vile right wing female in America, none other than Michelle Malkin, who attacked the author in her Twitchy blog on Sept. 9, 2012. Classic Conservative Attack!

Former leftist activist Lee Stranahan has been on the front lines in the fight against stalker and terrorist Brett Kimberlin. He and his family have recently been the victims of nasty threats from Kimberlin supporters and violent leftists, and, no longer feeling safe in their home, they have decided to flee. Blogger Aaron Walker, who has himself dealt with intimidation and lawfare, has more:

I have called and tweeted to him seeking a definitive statement about the cause. I will let you know if there is any definitive answer, but he would seem to be alluding to the recent threats of rape to himself and his wife by @Occupyrebellion who is definitely a member of Team Kimberlin and the Liberal Grouch (see here and here). (Update: read where Patrick quotes LG's language and see if that sounds like a threat to you)

And of course he has been viciously attacked by Brooks Bayne's crew for months.

Paddy Manning @**PaddyJManning** 6 Sep 12

@Stranahan That is shocking,horrible for you & your family.Courage,bad as this is, traumatic for your children,you know you light the dark

@PaddyJManning We're making the best of it and trying to look on the bright side.

Short Version: increasing intensity of the threats + public reveal of our address by a Kimberlin-y nut = problem **@AaronWorthing** **@rsmccain**

Over the weekend, Stranahan alerted police to one of the people making threats against him:

@LiberalGrouch I just spoke to as Sargent at the Howard County Police department. Go right ahead and call them, now, and prove your case.

Leftist and self-described "liberal patriot" Bill Schmalfeldt, aka The Liberal Grouch, has been among the most vocal of those threatening Stranahan. Here's just a brief sampling of his nastiness:

@OsborneInk ...he told the cops that I was threatening his wife and family. What the

fuck "tweet" is Pussy @Stranahan talking about???

Say, Gang! LET'S FIX LEE @Stranahan'S TEETH!!! - goo.gl/RmbgW via @Shareaholic

Scroll through his blog and Twitter feed at your own risk. He's truly vile.

Schmalfeldt insists he never made any threats:

I have never threatened harm, publicly or otherwise. 3 minutes.

As Patterico documented, Schmalfeldt's denial is patently false. Schmalfeldt insists that his threat was as innocuous as saying "good morning." Not remotely. Moreover, he repeatedly endorses and proclaims his solidarity with Twitterer @OccupyRebellion, another notorious Kimberlin supporter. @OccupyRebellion sent out a tweet clearly threatening Stranahan's wife:

While @Stranahan is in Tampa this week, should Texas rapists be told where to find his wife since he supports the rapes of everyone else?

Disgusting.

After receiving repeated threats of this nature, Stranahan feels his only remaining option is to move his family away from their current home. Doing so will require extra financial help. Stranahan took to Twitter to ask his supporters for assistance:

If you want to help out with these sudden moving expenses, you can send a donation via PayPal to stranahan@gmail.com

And, naturally, the vilest of the vile used Stranahan's financial hardships to mock him:

OK, you guys! Your boy needs your help with moving expenses. All you suckers pony up your hard earned bucks and give 'em to Scammy! #tcot

Seriously, even DULLEST conservative has to see Scammy for what he is now! Even YOU @aaronwalker and @joebrooks! Fucking shameless!

Baldfaced, toothless, shameless scam artists seeks help with moving expenses. Give all your money to his paypal! Do it NOW! #tlot #tcot

"Waaah. I'm Lee Stranahan and my family's lives are in danger. We have to move. Send me more donations!!"

Get a job & pay it yourself !!! RT @Stranahan If u want to help out with these sudden moving expenses, u can send donation via PayPal to ...

"Screw the family. They're just props. Send me more money. OUR LIVES ARE IN DANGER!!!!" -Stranahan

"I'm going to be sued, lose my kids, and end up in prison. This is great blogging material! I'll get more donations!!!!!!!" - Stranahan

It's utterly disgraceful. Thankfully, Stranahan is a far bigger man than all of his sick detractors combined, and he's vowed to keep his head up and fight the good fight:

If the left is fighting this hard to stop me, you have to assume I'm doing something right

Indeed. Meanwhile, you can also help Stranahan by remaining vigilant. And if you'd like to donate to the Bloggers Defense Fund, which goes toward aiding victims of Kimberlin-style lawfare, you can do so here.

Reminder: Stranahan remains under investigation for the possibility that one or more of the young women he photographed naked and in various stages of bondage may have been under 18-years old. He has also been exposed for (back when he was a liberal, of course) selling his wife (who he met on a porn shoot) to customers who would pay something like $200 to "pose" with her, and then would pay upwards of $600 to have her "personally deliver" the photographic prints in a two hour session where Lee and the kids would wait in the car while mommy was inside "delivering the prints."

If ever there ever was a man who was not prepared to die, it was Andrew Breitbart.

It was late on the evening of February 29, 2012. The Muckraker had a few drinks with a marketing director named Arthur Sando, a stranger he had just met, according to an article in the Hollywood Reporter.

"He was friendly and engaging," Sando recalled. "I said, 'You can't like the current slate of Republican candidates' and he said, 'Why would you say that?' I said, 'Well, they're talking about contraception,' and he said, 'The conversation is being framed by the liberal media.' I said, 'Well, the media isn't writing Rick Santorum's speeches for him.' We had a back-and-forth for awhile until we said we weren't going to agree on some things."

This friendly debate continued in the bar as the Muckraker sipped red wine, Sando said. "We just hit it off, he was delightful. There were other people who sat down and joined the conversation."

After about two hours of this friendly chit chat, the Muckraker decided it was time to amble on homeward. He exchanged contact info with Sando and was out the door.

He almost made it home. Less than an hour after exchanging business cards with Sando, in the very early hours of March 1, 2012, Andrew Breitbart was gradually assuming room temperature on a gurney in a Los Angeles area hospital.

If there is an afterlife for right wing muckrakers, and if Breitbart can see what's going on with his empire, what's being done in his name in the months after his sudden death, one has to wonder if he would be pleased.

Somehow, we don't think so.

A whole cottage industry has arisen based on "knowing Andrew" or "being associated with Andrew" or "having been converted from liberalism by Andrew." As you have seen in this telling of the tale, not all of these people who invoke Andrew Breitbart's name have his legacy as their primary concern.

There is a cancer in the former Andrew Breitbart body politic. How deep does it go? Has it gotten into the system where it can spread to the rest of the body? Or is it something that can be cut out, studied, learned from, and then saved in a laboratory of investigative journalism?

Of course, it wasn't cancer that killed Breitbart. It was his abused heart. But isn't hate kind of a cancer? When Breitbart died on March 1, 2012, did the cancer die with him?

Or was his death the thing that caused the cancer to spread? Every metastatic cancer has what's called a "sentinel node". That's the lymph node that indicates to the trained observer that the cancer has spread and something must be done if the patient is to be saved.

But is this patient one who CAN be saved? How widespread is the disease? Is it too late?

This cancer keeps popping up in one organ after another.

Now, it seems to have reached the office of the Los Angeles County District Attorney.

Let's examine the other organs to which this cancer has already been identified. After all, Breitbart had a wide circle of friends who also blogged in the conservative ether.

Aaron Walker and his pathological obsession with a crime committed some 40 years ago, where the criminal has served his time, paid his debt, and now wishes to live a quiet life as a liberal activist. Walker lost his job as a lawyer after he was the driving force behind the "Everyone Draw Mohammed Day" that caused widespread violence, death and destruction in the Middle East.

Robert Stacy McCain, who sobers up long enough to write anti-Semitic, racist diatribes that allegedly got him kicked out of a Seventh Day Adventist compound he once inhabited.

The rot-toothed turncoat Lee Stranahan, who was a liberal pornographer *(some of his photos are currently being investigated to see if the models were legally old enough to have naked bondage pictures taken of them),* who had a "Paul on the Road to Damascus" conversion after meeting Breitbart and is now one of the most obsequious, obnoxious, self-important publicity-seeking turds in the overflowing, filthy toilet of the Breitbart Memorial Empire.

And leave us not forget Patrick Frey.

Patrick Frey.

Patterico.

When the author was a federal employee (until March 2011 when my Parkinson's disease caused me to retire), he had to live under the constraints of the Hatch Act. At work, he was not allowed to write or say anything that promoted a partisan candidate, a political party, etc.

In his private writing, he had to make sure there was no connection between my official duties and my private thoughts.

How is it that a Deputy District Attorney in Los Angeles County is allowed to keep his job, living off the proceeds of county, state and federal taxes collected from the people of the county, the state of California and the taxpayers of the United States of America, when it turns out he was not only directly involved in what appears to be the commission of a crime, close association with a known criminal, and attempts to harass a person who claims sexual harassment at the hands of the above mentioned "known criminal"?

Deputy District Attorney, Patrick Frey, is also a well-known conservative blogger known as "Patterico." He blogs under the title "Patterico Pontificates." We have had our own mixups with Frey in the past, but those are not at issue now.

What is at issue, is this legal filing that alleges Mr. Frey and his wife, also of the District Attorney's office — both public servants — both officers of the court — two people who took an oath to "serve, protect and defend the

Constitution of America"– were not only friends with
convicted Breitbart hoaxter James O'Keefe (he of the
pimp costume, the fraudulent ACORN video, the attempt
to smear Shirley Sherrod at the USDA, and the event that
finally crossed the line — the attempt to tap into the
telephone lines of California Congresswoman Maxine
Waters), but may have KNOWN that O'Keefe intended
to break the law with his attempted wiretap of Rep.
Water's office in advance and failed to report it, as
required by a duly sworn officer of the court.

That's what's alleged in this court document, filed Oct. 2.

You can read the entire filing for yourself here. It's a
sordid affair, if true, of county officials using the power
of their offices to advance a partisan political agenda.
The filing alleges that Mr. Frey used his office to harass a
private citizen who may have been involved in a criminal
conspiracy with O'Keefe, who O'Keefe allegedly
drugged and tried to take sexual advantage of, and, in his
"Patterico Pontificates" blog, wrote alleged defamatory
and untrue things about the woman who attempted to
come forward to explain her connection with O'Keefe.
Again, read the entire filing. Then, ask yourself.

Would any of this nonsense be going on if Andrew Breitbart hadn't died? If "Daddy" was still running things in the Breitbart empire, would Lee Stranahan be under investigation for possible child pornography and pimping out his own wife? Would Ali Akbar be sending out chuckling little tweets, reeking of his own hubris, about how he is untouchable by law? Would the National Bloggers' Club have done things legally if Breitbart had lived, or would they have pretended to be a legitimate 501(c)3, which they are not?

And while we're at it.

If Breitbart were still alive, would he have pulled back the reins on people like the besotted R. Stacy McCain ("The OTHER McCain")? Would he have, by now, told Aaron Walker (Worthing?) to shut his cake hole and get a job? Would Michelle Malkin have sought the services of the American Center for Law and Justice to "defend" Ali Akbar and the National Bloggers Club, or would she have known that there was at least one alleged rotten apple in the ACLJ barrel in the form of former ACLJ senior counsel and Regent University Adjunct Law Professor James M. Henderson, Sr., who was either forced to resign, was fired, or for whatever reason has been erased from all memory on the ACLJ website since this blog and Exposed Politics made public the allegations that the married father of eight was involved in exchanging money, alcohol and drugs in exchange for being on the receiving end of anal sex with a variety of young men over the last few years, at least one of which we have established was not quite 18 when Henderson, under an assumed name (that didn't fool his victims — if his over-18 year old paramours can be called victims — legally, in Virginia, the age of consent is 18)?

Would Breitbart, who was addled but not crazy and certainly not stupid, have made sure he surrounded himself with people who were trustworthy? Or does his drunken rant videotaped shortly before his death, screaming "STOP RAPING PEOPLE", only apply to liberals?

I'm no doctor, although I did play one on the radio.

This cancer has spread to far too many organs for this patient to survive. You can smell the rot, seeping through the pores. Each breath has the sickeningly sweet stench of decay. The body is a shell, more tumor than useful tissue at this point.

SOMEBODY needs to come to the realization that this cancer has spread too far to be cured.

It's time to pull the plug.

But then, according to a story by McKay Coppins in Buzz Feed the decomposing corpse of Andrew Breitbart, having been picked clean by the carrion-eating parasites that have made their homes in his carcass, may be collapsing under its own weight. (http://www.buzzfeed.com/mckaycoppins/breitbarts-inheritors-battle-over-his-legacy)

"...insiders say that a few strong months of traffic, aided by regular, loyal Drudge links, have masked deeper problems. The portrait that emerged from multiple interviews with sources at the site and in its orbit was one of a disorganized, downtrodden army of conservative foot soldiers eager to carry out their fallen leader's mission, but deeply divided over how to interpret his battle plan.

"We were running a kind of happy cult when Andrew was in charge, and when Andrew died everyone had an incentive to spin what they thought he was up to," said one former employee. "If he knew he was going to die, I'm sure he would have called a dinner the night before and given us the tablets or something.... But he didn't."

Would Big Daddy Andy be happy with the laughing stock his children have created in his name?

"I don't even call it Breitbart.com anymore," said one staffer. "I call it Wannabe Breitbart.com. I said at the time, when Andrew died, they gotta shut this thing down or else it's going to fall apart. I think I was right."

If the increasingly unhinged nature of his Tweeting is any indication...

Ali A. Akbar @ali   11h
Today I was driving and I thought to myself, "I'm done with soda."
Looking forward to being healthier again.
Expand

Ali Abdul Razaq Akbar is running neck and neck with Breitbart.com in the race to obscurity. If it can be proven that laws were broken in his pursuit of the "lost ark of political relevance," Akbar's story could wind up coming full circle. And this time, it will be hard time. No probation.

Stay tooned.

ABOUT THE AUTHOR

Bill Schmalfeldt retired from his storied career as a
broadcaster, editor, reporter, award-winning columnist,
talk show host and writer/editor for the Federal
Government when his Parkinson's disease progressed to
the point where he could no longer tolerate the commute
from his home south of Baltimore to his office in
Bethesda, Maryland. He keeps his mind busy by
blogging at the Patriot-Ombudsman (http://patriot-
ombudsman.com) and you can tweet up a storm with him
at http://twitter.com/patriotombud. He has authored
several books of political satire as well as first-hand
accounts about his struggle with Parkinson's disease, all
which can be found at Amazon.com.

Image by Barbara Broido

OTHER BOOKS BY BILL SCHMALFELDT

(All available at all major online booksellers)

DEEP BRAIN DIARY

NO DOORWAY WIDE ENOUGH

YOU NEVER MISS THE DOPAMINE (Until the Brain Runs Dry, Vol. I & II)

PUT ON YOUR PARKY FACE

"...by the people..."

HUNKY DUNK

UNDERCOVER TRUCKER (How I Saved America by Truckin' Towels for the Taliban)

END TIMES (A play, written with my late twin brother, Bob Schmalfeldt)

OUTRAGEOUS ACCUSATIONS AND DAMNABLE LIES

WHY I HATE AMERICA, FREEDOM AND EVERYTHING DECENT

CAN YOU BE A TEA PARTY MEMBER AND STILL CALL YOURSELF A CHRISTIAN?

UNCLE BILL'S BEDTIME STORIES FOR PROGRESSIVES

UNZIPPING THE MITT

EATING BREITBART

Made in the USA
Middletown, DE
30 October 2020

23059313R00133